GROWTH AMIDST

DECLINE

WHAT THE 2016 SCOTTISH CHURCH CENSUS REVEALED

GROWTH AMIDST DECLINE

WHAT THE 2016 SCOTTISH CHURCH CENSUS REVEALED

Peter Brierley

Publishers
2017

ADBC Publishers,
The Old Post Office,
1, Thorpe Avenue, Tonbridge,
Kent TN10 4PW
United Kingdom

www.brierleyconsultancy.com

First published June, 2017
Copyright © Peter Brierley, 2017

Cover design by David McNeill, Revo Creative
Maps drawn by Orange and Blue

Edited by Rosemary Dowsett

Typeset by Graham Stacey, Orange and Blue

Printed in Great Britain by Bell & Bain, Glasgow

ISBN-13:   978-0-9957646-0-6

DEDICATION

To my wife of over 50 years, Cherry,
without whose constant support,
encouragement and willingness to
help in every way possible, this
analysis would never have been
finished nor the book completed.
She has been totally wonderful
and with unbounded patience!

THANKS

Many have helped with this study, the inspiration for which began in the University of Glasgow in 2013. From there it was enthusiastically taken up by a small number who remembered the value of the previous Church Census in 2002, especially Rev Dr Fergus MacDonald, a past Moderator of the Free Church of Scotland, and Rev Colin Sinclair, Senior Minister of Palmerston Place Church in Edinburgh, Chair of the 2002 Steering Committee and who very kindly served again as Chair of the 2016 Steering Committee. The study owes a huge amount to the commitment of these two men and all their wisdom and advice in sorting out the way we should go. Grateful thanks also for the hospitality of Elaine Duncan, Chief Executive of the Scottish Bible Society, who allowed the Steering Committee to meet in their board Room. The members of the Steering Committee are given in the text and we are very grateful to them for all the support and helpful discussions that took place. Likewise to the representatives of the organisations which sponsored questions in the Census, which enabled it to be viable – Alpha Scotland, Tearfund Scotland, Christian Aid Scotland and the University of Edinburgh – and without whose support it would not have happened. I would also like to thank John Marcus for his computer expertise, crucial to the project, Kim Tainio for wrestling with SPSS to obtain many analyses, Lynn Allen and a small team filling and posting thousands of letters, and especially to Lynn for her seemingly endless data input, Rose Dowsett for incredible eagle-eyed proof reading, and many others involved in every possible way. While the mistakes remain my responsibility, the project as a whole to bring this to a successful conclusion is the work of many committed people, to all of whom a HUGE vote of thanks!

Contents

INTRODUCTION

It was a Scottish initiative! The University of Glasgow held a Round Table Seminar in September 2013 at which one of the presentations was, by their request, a brief discussion of the results of the previous Scottish Church Censuses which had been held in 1984, 1994 and 2002, and whether a fourth should be held. This led to a conclusion indicating a further Census could be helpful. That desire was followed up initially by correspondence with the denominational leaders present at that Seminar.

The outcome was a meeting with a larger number of denominational leaders present, held in Edinburgh in October 2014. After a brief introductory presentation of what kind of results a Census finds, if like the previous ones, the concept of a further similar Census, having been outlined in a previously circulated proposal, was discussed in some detail (its methodology, timing, costs), and whether such might be supported by the churches. A number of suggested changes were made (such as using email where possible instead of paper post to reduce costs), and a revised proposal was requested, which was accepted at a further meeting of the same group the following February. It was also agreed that Brierley Consultancy should be asked to undertake the study since its Principal had been responsible for all three of the previous Censuses.

The costs were also agreed, with more being contributed by the Church of Scotland and the Roman Catholic Church than the smaller denominations. It was also agreed that various (charitable) organisations should be approached with a view to sponsoring questions to make up that part of the total costs (about a quarter) which the denominations were unable to pay, analogous to what had happened with previous Censuses.

Those who were kind enough to serve on the Steering Committee were as follows, being joined by Lt Col Carol Bailey the Scottish Office Secretary of the Salvation Army for the final meetings:

Rev Colin Sinclair, then Convener, Mission and Discipleship Council, Church of Scotland, but also Senior Minister, Palmerston Church [Chair]

Mr Gordon Bell, Communications Officer, Free Church of Scotland (on behalf of Rod Morrison, Chief Administration Officer) initially, but later Rev David Meredith, Mission Director
Father Thomas Boyle, Assistant General Secretary, The (Roman Catholic) Bishops' Conference of Scotland
Rev Alan Donaldson, General Director, Baptist Union of Scotland
Rev John Fulton, General Secretary, United Free Church of Scotland
Rev John Humphrey, Moderator, United Reformed Church, Synod of Scotland who sadly died while the Census was progressing, and was replaced as Moderator by Rev David Pickering
Rev Canon Fay Lamont, Scottish Episcopal Church (on behalf of Rev John Stuart, Secretary General)
Rev Dr Fergus Macdonald, former Moderator, Free Church of Scotland
Dr Alastair Noble, The Christian Brethren
Rev Dr Fiona Tweedie, Mission Statistics Co-ordinator, Church of Scotland

The organizations which agreed to support the Census by sponsoring questions were the University of Edinburgh, Tearfund Scotland, Christian Aid and Scottish Alpha.

The broad methodology followed is described in the Appendix, and Census Sunday was designated as Sunday, 8th May 2016 (services held on the previous Saturday also being counted). The questionnaire used is given in *UK Church Statistics* No 3 2018 Edition.[1] This report gives the findings from this Census, compares them with answers from previous Censuses where applicable, and also the results of the sponsored questions, though each of the sponsoring organisations has in addition subsequently received a more detailed report of their questions for their management purposes.

Executive Summary

The Church Census held in May 2016 was the fourth Census which has been undertaken of Scottish Church attendance, the first being held in 1984, thus giving an overall time frame of 32 years. Each has encompassed a variety of factors, but has especially focused on congregational numbers attending a place of Christian worship on a Sunday. The 2016 Census showed that some 390,000 people regularly attended church, being 7.2% of the Scottish population, down from 17% in 1984. This report makes it easier for the church to focus on numbers or other aspects of church life rather than on the mission of the church, but the detail hopefully will be a stimulus to the fulfilment of this divine commission. "The exercise was certainly well worthwhile and has given us some food for thought," wrote one respondent.[2]

A significant finding was the decline in all denominations except for the Pentecostals where attendance has almost doubled since the third Census in 2002 and stands at 19,000, 5% of all Scottish churchgoers in 2016. However, many immigrant churches (called "Overseas National" churches in this report) and Messy Churches have also started in the last 10 years, so this is not a pessimistic story of inevitable decline.

Growth

Many of the new churches have the characteristics of being led by local lay people, often without theological training, informality in worship, sometimes food, certainly a warm welcome, full fellowship, enterprise, borrowing of premises, with a deep concern for reaching out to others and making sure the worship service is relevant and in the appropriate language! Some 12,000 people regularly attend some 300 new churches started since 2002.

In addition a number of congregations (over 500) reported significant growth over the last five years, leading to an additional 6,000 people in church each Sunday. Over 52,000 children also now attend church who weren't born in 2002 (6% of all births), making a total of at least 70,000 new people in Scottish church life, 1.3% of the population.

The growth that has been seen has caused the previously expected decline to moderate, and, although the future trend remains downwards, numbers could fall to just under 300,000 by 2025 if the present trend continues. Across Scotland the main growth was seen in Aberdeenshire largely because of the number of Polish immigrants, mostly Roman Catholic, employed in the oil industry.

Congregations

The Census has focused on congregations rather than churches per se as a number of church mergers have taken place in the last few years without the usual closure of some church buildings. The number of congregations in 2016 was 3,700, down from 4,100 in 1984. While over 300 churches have started in Scotland since 2002, this has been offset by a greater number of closures. Nearly half, 46%, of congregations acknowledged decline in the last 5 years (Table 2.10). The average congregation in 2016 was 105, but 15% were over 200 (Table 2.13). The decrease in numbers is equivalent to losing 10 congregations per month.

Two-fifths, 40%, of the churches (as given by their minister) were Evangelical (Table 5.1), up from 38% in 1994 (not measured in 1984), while 24% were Broad/Liberal, 17% were Reformed, 13% Catholic. A large proportion of churches in current use were built in the 19th (30%) or 20th (47%) centuries, with 9% of congregations started since the year 2000. These latter were either Church of Scotland mergers or new Independent, Pentecostal or Smaller Denominational (which included Messy Church) churches (Table 9.1).

Age and gender of churchgoers

A key finding from this Census was that two-fifths, 42%, of Scottish churchgoers are 65 or over, of which a fifth are aged 65 to 74, and a fifth 75 or over. This is twice the proportion in the population, and has obvious implications for the future. Two-fifths of churchgoers, 40%, are male (Table 3.1), slightly more than the 37% in 1984. The oldest churchgoers are either in the Church of Scotland or Scottish Episcopal Church, the youngest are Pentecostal or among the Smaller Denominations group (Table 3.8). Declining numbers are especially seen in those under 45 (Figure 3.11).

Other characteristics of Scottish churchgoers

Four-fifths, 80%, attend weekly, the remaining fifth less frequently (Figure 4.1), those aged 35-44 attending less often. 4% of those in church on Census Sunday in 2016 were visitors. An extra 3% of the population attend church at Christmas, especially in Church of Scotland and Roman Catholic churches. A large majority, 94%, of Scottish churchgoers were White, with half the other 6% being Black (four times the population proportion). These latter were mainly aged 25 to 34 and Pentecostal.

Almost half, 45%, of churchgoers had been in their present church for over 20 years (Table 4.8), and half, 50%, lived between ½ and 3 miles from their church (Table 4.13). A third, 35%, of all churchgoers (counting congregational numbers as against churches) were Evangelical (Table 5.1), up from 26% in 1994, while another third, 32%, were Catholic, with 16% Broad/ Liberal (twice as many women as men), 13% Reformed, and 4% Low Church. Catholics and Charismatic Evangelicals were the youngest (Table 5.7). As might be expected, particular parts of Scotland tended to be dominated by certain denominations.

Leadership

Four-fifths of church leaders, 79%, are male, with an average age of 57. They have been leading their present church usually for 8 years (11 if Pentecostal); those serving their current church longest were either in Dumfries & Galloway, Dundee, North Ayrshire or the Shetland Islands.

Two-fifths, 43%, were responsible for more than one church, especially those in Roman Catholic, Scottish Episcopal, Church of Scotland or Methodist churches. Those serving in urban areas were less likely to have such responsibilities. One ninth, 11%, of churches had a youth-worker, 4% full-time, 7% part-time.

Mid-week attendance

Three-fifths, 60%, of churches had some kind of mid-week worship, especially Pentecostal, Roman Catholic and Baptist churches. Average attendance was 34, up from 27 in 2002, and younger than those who come on a Sunday (Figure 8.3). Most, 89%, also came on a Sunday.

Half of all churches, 48%, held a mid-week youth activity, with an average attendance of 41, down from 59 in 2002 (Table 8.6). Only two-fifths, 42%, of these also came on a Sunday. Half of all churches, 46%, also held other kinds of mid-week ministry, with an average attendance of 51, slightly fewer men, again younger than Sunday attendees, although these were not Sunday churchgoers.

Together the mid-week work reached almost a quarter of a million people, 235,000, of whom three-fifths, 58%, did not attend on a Sunday (Table 8.10), giving **a total reach of 10%** of the Scottish population coming to church either on a Sunday or mid-week.

Local Community

Sponsored questions showed that three-quarters, 72%, of churches sought to meet local social needs and half, 48%, undertook regular neighbourhood visitation (Table 10.1). A third of churches, 35%, had undertaken an Alpha course, half (17%) in 2015, giving a total of 940 courses run that year. This included Youth Alpha as well as Adult Alpha, with an average attendance of 12 each. *Christianity Explored* courses had been taken by 10% of Scottish churches (Table 10.4).

Three-quarters, 77%, of churches supported charities if they could direct their donation to a specific project or place, the most important factor, however, being whether the purpose to which it was going fitted in with the church's vision (Table 10.5). A third, 34%, of churches had been involved with Tearfund, and three-fifths, 61%, with Christian Aid Week. Poverty reduction was well supported, environmental conservation was much lobbied (Table 10.7). A quarter, 24%, of churches had raised the topic of legacies.

The Census provides much information. A special section starting on page 171 suggests how individual local congregations might use some of the findings. Senior leadership will wish to consider the strategic implications of the key findings about the rate of decline, the serious age factor, and the undoubted fact that within overall decline there are definite shoots of growth along mostly non-traditional lines.

Will formality, rules, inflexible structures, resistance to innovation, tradition and rigid denominationalism hinder these shoots of growth or adapt to encompass them?

Peter Brierley
May 2017

1

WHY HAVE ANOTHER CHURCH CENSUS?

The first Census to be held in Britain was the Population Census of 1801, followed every ten years of those ending in "1" until 1941 when it was deferred because of WWII. The first Church Census took place as part of the 1851 Population Census in England and Wales. It focussed on attendance at each of the (up to) three services then held in most churches on a Sunday and the number of seats available for the congregation. It did not look at total attendance. An attempt was made to undertake a Census of the churches in what is now Greater London in 1886 and 1903, but was limited to the capital.

The first national Church Census was undertaken across England in 1979 by the British and Foreign Bible Society, under Rev Tom Houston, at that time requiring attendance information, as opposed to membership, of the churches for a large Nationwide Initiative in Evangelism Conference which took place in Nottingham in September 1980. The results of this study stimulated similar censuses in Wales in 1982 and Scotland in 1984. A second English Church Census was held in 1989 and obtained a response of 70% from the 38,000 churches it approached.

A further Scottish Church Census was undertaken in 1994, and used similar questions on churchmanship and environment as had the English one in 1989. It was based on a comprehensive address list and achieved a better response rate than the previous Census in 1984. Further studies in England followed in 1998 and 2005 and in Scotland in 2002. A London Church Census was held in 2012.

The value of having a series of such Censuses means that the concept is not foreign to most ministers, and there is often a goodwill factor in being willing to participate in a national exercise, especially if a summary of results is promised free to all who participate as a kind of tangible token of gratitude for the time and effort taken in their completing the original form. It also means that the past results can be used as a broad predictor for the future.

The basic data files, anonymised, of all the Censuses held since the Welsh Census of 1982 have been lodged with the Data Archive at the University of Essex.

Why consider another Census?

Scotland's population is growing: it was 5.3 million when measured in the government Population Census in 2011, up 5% on the 5.1 million in 2001. However, within that growth, the *religious make-up of the population is changing quite rapidly*: while Christians were two-thirds, 65%, of the population in 2001, they were only just over half, 54%, ten years later, because many will have died in the inter-censal decade and not been replaced.

As Christians have declined, so has *the mix within that category*, as shown by the different denominations in the civil Census counts. It may be seen from Table 1.1 that the Church of Scotland has declined quite considerably, but the Roman Catholics have stayed the same percentage, any decline in their numbers being probably offset by the influx of immigrants from Catholic countries in Europe.

Table 1.1: Percentage of the Scottish population by Religion and Denomination

Religion	2001	2011	Denomination	2001	2011
Christian	65	54	Roman Catholic	16	16
Muslim	1	1	Presbyterian	42	33
Other religions	1	1	Anglican	3	2
No Religion	28	37	Other excl. Ang	4	3
Not stated	5	7	Christian Total	65	54
Base (=100%)	5.1 m	5.3 m			

The civil Census, however, only measures adherents. The decline in adherence shown in the Table is naturally of concern, but how far *have the changes over recent years been reflected in church attendance*, for example?

Has attendance also declined to the same extent and, if it has, *has such occurred equally* across all age-groups, both genders, over the different local government Councils in Scotland? It is the numbers coming to church that make up the practical arm of the church in terms of voluntary service to the community, as well as being the heart of the worshipping numbers and the key to growth. While ticking "Christian" on a national census form gives an idea of people's religious sympathies, it is largely through church attendance that Christian commitment can be assessed.

There are other reasons why another Scottish Church Census would be valuable. As well as demographic, immigration, and denominational change, has the political change in Scotland over recent years impacted church attendance? Society is also rapidly changing, the impact of which on church life needs to be assessed, particularly in terms of encouraging and stimulating growth.

The broad results of the previous Scottish Church Censuses have shown that church attendance in Scotland is much higher than in England: 17% of the population in 1984 compared with 10% in England in 1989, but it had dropped to 11% in Scotland in 2002. Is the rate of decline accelerating or slowing? It takes a long time to turn a big ship round, and *a knowledge of the rate of change as well as the extent of change is important*. More, and perhaps different, information may be required to determine the best actions for the future.

How far has any change in numbers impacted young people, for example? "Church Without Walls" was very prominent at the time of the last Church Census in 2002 – is it still an important element in congregational growth? It is easy to think that certain changes are occurring because of one observed change in one part of Scotland. The value of a Census is to measure change simultaneously in *all areas and across all denominations*.

The English church scene in its 2005 Census revealed a number of areas of concern, especially the decline in youth numbers. The London Church Census, on the other hand, showed growth across the capital, largely because of the impact of immigration. How far has change in numbers of *young people, and patterns of migration*, impacted the church in Scotland? Has the urban change seen in London been replicated in, say, Glasgow and Edinburgh? Such comparative information is important, as evangelistic decline in one group might be ameliorated by success elsewhere, such as perhaps in "Messy Church".

There is also another challenge, which comes from *a measure of churchmanship*. Not every group in either England in 2005 or London in 2012 changed in the same way over the previous period. In London the evangelicals were growing in many Boroughs. Are evangelicals growing also in Scotland or, as in England overall, are they also declining? In London the charismatics are an especially important group because of their rapid growth. Are they growing in Scotland also and, if so, what can be learned from them which might help others to experience growth?

The Value of such Censuses

What value have previous Scottish Church Censuses been and what is the potential value of a fourth Church Census in Scotland?

1. They measure basic numerical strength. They give essential statistics to every church leader who wishes to have them, allowing him/her to compare their data with Council and other secular data, and allow their own denominational data to be compared with other Scottish denominational data. They provide an overview of denominational strength.

2. They give an overview of trends. They indicate the likely future, should present trends continue, and show likely changes at Council level, hopefully giving needed encouragement to leaders in difficult areas. They also help identify the impact of Christianity on Scottish society in general.
3. They help local church leaders to plan strategically not only for themselves but in unity with other local church leaders. A fuller picture of what is happening church-wise within each Council is given.

Thus a Scottish Church Census provides the opportunity for existing or emerging leadership to take appropriate actions. So why was a further Scottish Church Census held in 2016?

1. *Scotland is rapidly changing*. There is much population movement and immigration which impacts the country. Not all newcomers, even Christian newcomers, end up regularly attending church. There are also denominational changes taking place, with new denominations being started in Scotland, and a new leadership style is in place in some churches. There is also a great deal of political activity at this time.
2. *Comparisons may be made*. Changes in Scotland can be compared with other changes. There is an evangelistic need to reach many in Scotland. The Census allows comparisons between Scotland and other countries, and between urban centres and London, for example.
3. *A baseline* for future changes will be established, likely to be of critical use in evaluating the Scottish Bible Society's *Transforming Scotland* project,[3] and supplement the data in the Church of Scotland and other denominations' church-finder websites, help in the understanding of the data on religion from the national Censuses of Population published by the National Records of Scotland, and enable other research to be seen in a national context of attendance.

So in summary what should another Scottish Church Census actually do? It would:

- Give a current up-to-date pattern of church attendance (by gender, age-group, church ethos, ethnicity and geography) throughout Scotland
- Give a detailed local picture of attendance available by Scottish Council
- Suggest pointers for identified past growth or decline
- Update long-term trends (across 30 years) and allow future trends to be more firmly estimated
- Provide strategic data for local and ecumenical leadership
- Give comprehensive information on church life throughout Scotland
- Measure midweek activity, fringe meetings, community action, informal church, and youth information in greater detail
- Assess the impact that especially large churches are making
- Be a valuable catalyst for seeking further information
- Be a model or pattern or yardstick for other countries to follow should they wish.

The date chosen for the Census, Sunday May 8th, 2016, was chosen because it was not a Bank Holiday weekend, nor was it during the school holidays, not in the winter when inclement weather can lessen numbers going to church, but it was as average a Sunday as any. If any church found that that particular Sunday was awkward for their programme (perhaps it was a Communion Sunday, for example, or one having baptisms), churches were welcome to substitute an alternative date for their Census, and a number did so. (The very slight statistical error introduced by this timing difference is inconsequential).

It will be noticed that this date follows almost two years after the Scottish Referendum of 2014 when the population voted whether to remain within the United Kingdom (doing so by 55% to 45%), but came just before the UK Referendum on whether to remain or leave the European Union (the result of which was 52% Leave and 48% Remain, although Scotland as a whole voted to Remain with 62%[4]).

The following chapters analyse the Census results, looking at the key control variables initially and then the remainder of the questions.

2

THE NUMBER ATTENDING CHURCH

Many churches replied to the Census, and a number of ministers or other leaders, such as the Clerk of Synod or the Vestry Secretary,[5] clearly went to a great deal of trouble to ensure that information given for their church was as accurate as possible. Several wrote very helpful explanatory letters in addition, or included notes to indicate how their answers were achieved or why a particular number was exceptionally high (church held a baptism) or low (people were on holiday) on that particular Sunday. The Planning Committee is enormously grateful for the time and concern many respondents took. Several leaders in churches with large congregations, say over 200, took especial care to ensure that all their numbers added up correctly. This kind of support for a major initiative is hugely appreciated, and one can only impersonally thank those so much for their help in ensuring that the Census data is as good as it could be.

Unfortunately not every church replied to the Census. In total, data was available from 40% of the 3,689 churches in Scotland, and total attendance is grossed up from the total given by those congregations. The number is statistically sufficient to give valid results. However, the total is not simply a process of increasing the number from the forms by a single division to estimate what is 100%, since that can bring in a biased figure. What if, say, all the churches in one denomination replied but very few in another? Simply grossing up would not then give a correct estimate of the total. So the total replies given for each denomination were taken, and each was individually grossed up, giving a grand total in one dimension. The same exercise was also undertaken by churchmanship and by Council area, to give two further estimates. Each of these totals gave slightly different answers, discussed below.

Congregations not churches

There is also a problem of nomenclature. The Church of Scotland, the Scottish Episcopal Church, the Roman Catholic Church and some smaller denominations are taking the administrative decision to merge some of their parishes, usually, say, merging two or three churches into one single congregation, normally with just a single minister. This is mostly the result of individual churches being no longer financially viable, or there not being sufficient ministers for there to be one per church, so pastoral oversight is continued by providing one person to share their ministry among two or more congregations.

Some of the merged churches are then formally closed, which is straightforward. In other situations, however, the various united congregations do not wish to see their church building closed and the new combined worshiping congregation begins a pattern of moving from one church to another, usually on alternate weeks, for their worship, thus keeping the various church buildings in use. Such churches thus remain usable and open but the congregation no longer meets in them every week.

For Census purposes these not-regularly-used-every-week churches are treated as if they were closed, since no congregation actually used it on Census Sunday. The Census is actually focusing on *congregations* not churches, although the use of the word "church" to mean a "worshiping congregation" is very widespread, and will be used in this report on many occasions. It does mean, however, that the number of congregations in a particular denomination will be less than the number of churches for which it is responsible (and which are open and used occasionally), and it is the congregational total, not the church total, which is used here for grossing up to get total attendance.

Denominational groupings

There are 83 distinct denominations in Scotland of which the largest three are the Church of Scotland (41% of total congregations), the Roman Catholic Church (13%) and the

Scottish Episcopal Church (8%). It will be noted that these three form over three-fifths, 61%, of all the congregations in Scotland. The remainder are numerous, and are listed in detail in *UK Church Statistics*.

The situation is similar to the other countries constituting the United Kingdom, which had a total of almost 300 different denominations in 2015, and for convenience these are broken down into 10 broad divisions which have been used for many years in books like the *UK Christian Handbook, Religious Trends* and now continued in *UK Church Statistics*. The denominational groups in Scotland largely follow these 10 divisions, but keep the Church of Scotland which is the largest single denomination, as well as being the National Church, separate from the other Presbyterian churches which are grouped together as "Other Presbyterians". The previous Censuses divided the data into 7 denominational categories as follows:

Table 2.1: Denominational groups used in the 2016 Scottish Church Census

- **Church of Scotland**
- **Other Presbyterian** churches (including the Free Church of Scotland, United Free Church of Scotland, Free Church of Scotland [Continuing],Free Presbyterian Church of Scotland, Associated Presbyterian Churches, other Presbyterian Churches, and the United Reformed Church, one of whose initiating partners was a Presbyterian Church)
- **Episcopal** (the Scottish Episcopal Church, formerly the Episcopal Church of Scotland [Anglican])
- **Baptist** Churches (Baptist Union, Grace Baptist and Independent Baptists)
- **Independent Churches** (the New/"House" Churches and their various streams, Christian Brethren [Open and Exclusive], Congregational Churches, Fellowship of Churches of Christ, Fellowship of Independent Evangelical Churches [FIEC] and other independent churches)
- **Smaller Denominations** (Fresh Expressions [or Messy

Church etc] across the various denominations but included here as a single unit, Methodists, Orthodox, Salvation Army, Lutheran, Nazarenes, Pentecostal denominations, Quakers, Local Ecumenical Projects (LEPs), Seventh-Day Adventist, Worldwide Church of God, various Immigrant Churches, Military Chaplaincies and others)

• **Roman Catholic** Churches (including a few immigrant Ukrainian and Polish Catholic congregations).

However, over the 14 years since 2002, a number of changes have taken place. One of these is the increasing number of "Fresh Expressions" (described in more detail below), the reduction of the number of LEPs, the cessation of many military chaplains who are not now holding regular services in Armed Forces bases, the change of name of the Worldwide Church of God to Grace Communion International, as well as the significant increase in the number of immigrant and Pentecostal denominations. Most of these changes mean that the "Smaller Denominations" category used in the 2016 analysis is not constituted in quite the same way as hitherto.

In particular the increase in Pentecostal and Charismatic Immigrant groups is such that their importance means they need to form a separate eighth category, not used before, and whose numbers for previous years will be estimated from earlier Censuses. This means we need to add to the above:

• **Pentecostal** Churches (Assemblies of God, Redeemed Christian Church of God, Elim Pentecostal, New Testament Church of God, Apostolic Church, Struthers Memorial Churches, United Pentecostal Church of Great Britain & Ireland, Mountain of Fire Ministries, Potters House Christian Fellowship, Church of Pentecost, Destiny Churches of Christ, United Pentecostal Church of Great Britain and other Pentecostal churches).

Some of these smaller Pentecostal denominations are relatively new to the Scottish scene. The largest, the Redeemed Christian Church of God, came from Nigeria initially, starting in Britain in 1988 but has planted over 700 churches in the last 20 years throughout the UK with 64% of our cities and towns having such a church. Their motto is "a church within 10 minutes walking distance of where people live," something which comes straight out of rural Nigeria where people are unable to catch buses or take cars to church! It is strategically led by Pastor Agu Irukwu, who is the minister of the 3,000+ strong congregation at Jesus House for all Nations in Brent in west London.

The Mountain of Fire Ministries, Potters House, and the Church of Pentecost are also all new in Scotland in recent years, each having about 100 congregations throughout the UK. They are all West African churches which can be described as "reverse mission," churches desiring to see the evangelisation of Britain whose African mother churches feel that the British churches have lost the cutting edge of the Gospel. The Destiny Church is also a new Pentecostal denomination which originated in Glasgow in the 1990s.[6]

Church Without Walls and Fresh Expressions

"Church Without Walls" was the name given to a report presented to the Church of Scotland General Assembly in May 2001 by the Special Commission anent Review and Reform. The report, by convener Rev Peter Neilson,[7] sought to encourage greater evangelism within the local communities of churches. While the concept began as a Church of Scotland initiative, it spread to other denominations and was formally incorporated into the Fresh Expression movement a few years ago.

Analogous to this movement, but initially completely separate from it, was the formation in 2005 of "Fresh Expressions," under former Archbishop Rowan Williams of the Church of England, in succession to his predecessor's "Springboard" initiative which he didn't wish to continue. Fresh Expressions aimed to encourage new groups of people, especially those not normally attending church, to come together to think and consider the Christian faith, often meeting in a non-ecclesial environment such as a village hall or local school, and invariably including a meal or food of some description. Often led by lay people, though encouraged by the ordained minister in a parish, the movement became very popular and quickly spread to other denominations, especially the Methodists, Baptists, Salvation Army and the Roman Catholics.

Fresh Expressions was initially led by Bishop Graham Cray, former Principal of Ridley Theological College in Cambridge, who then was succeeded by Steve Croft, now Bishop of Oxford. It is now led by Canon Phil Potter. Although technically Fresh Expressions dates from 2005, the name has come to include all the other types of informal church, including those which were started perhaps many years before 2005. 1992 is now usually taken as the starting point and Church Without Walls is a formal part of it. Fresh Expressions aims to be a group of people meeting regularly (usually at least once a month, but some in Scotland meet bi-monthly) with the intention of eventually becoming a formal church. Not all succeed in becoming a regular or growing meeting, but many do. The general experiment is watched eagerly by others, as in Australia, seeking to identify new contemporary models of church.[8]

Some of these fellowships were previously called by other names like Mission-minded Churches, Pub or Café Churches, and a new group called "Messy Church" started in 2008, but they are all more simply called under the umbrella collective title of "Fresh Expressions." Messy Churches are a major component of Fresh Expressions, which have been helped enormously by the Bible Reading Fellowship sponsoring a Messy Church officer, Lucy Moore, who produces many publications for their use as well as keeping a list of those churches with such groups. For Census purposes a separate code was allocated for Fresh Expressions/Messy Churches, and will be analysed specially later, but they are included as part of "Smaller Denominations" even though most of them have a specific denominational base, often the Church of Scotland or Salvation Army, but are retained under this grouping as these congregations are not generally separately counted within the denomination from which they sprang. Some 392 Messy Churches were listed in Scotland in

2013,[9] but the detailed website contains only a fifth of these, 21%, although all those which were listed were sent Census forms. Results from them are given in Chapter 9.

Café churches also continue. "We now have a Café Church in our Village Hall instead of worship in church a few Sundays each year," wrote one respondent who ministered to two rural congregations in the Scottish Borders.[10] He found this outreach "a strategic way in contacting and involving a younger age group" which is "quietly helping us see what the church in the future is likely to be like." Such may also help in the formation of "Community Hubs" seeking to represent communities of around 1,000 people, including church networks and pastors as well as education services, the business sector, local government and others.[11]

Churchmanship and Area Codes

The other two main "control" variables, as they are called, used for Census purposes were (a) the churchmanship and (b) locational area in which a church was situated. Most questions are analysed by these two factors also, and are used for analysis of other questions in Chapters 4 and 6 respectively.

Total Scottish Church Attendance in 2016

Altogether data came from 40% of the 3,689 congregations in Scotland in 2016.[12] The total attendance on or around Census Sunday of 8th May was **389,510 people**, which rounds to 390,000, which is 7.2% of the population.[13] This figure is derived from a comparison of those obtained by grossing up for churches not replying by denomination, by churchmanship and by the geographical area in which a church was located. This is not the total number of Christians in Scotland (2.9 million according to the 2011 Census [Table 1.1]), but it will certainly exclude the thousands in the "invisible church" researched by Steve Aisthorpe.[14]

A considerable number of churches, of the order of 39% of the churches then existing in 2002,[15] replied in 2002 but didn't reply in 2016. Some of these will have closed in the interim, so their total 2002 attendance will be less in 2016 (a) because of those closures and (b) will have participated in the general decline anyway. However, these figures were also used in the assessment of the total just given.

The 1984 Scottish Census recorded total church attendance as 854,000, and between 1984 and 2002 it reduced by 33.2% to 570,000 in 2002. That 2002 attendance figure has reduced over 14 years to 390,000 in 2016, a reduction of 31.7%. These figures indicate two very similar falls in total church attendance on a typical Sunday, though the first was over 18 years and the second over 14 years. That difference in period will mean that the average per annum rate of decline will be slightly different, being -2.2% per annum for the first period and -2.7% for the second period.

Better than expected

The result of the 2016 Scottish Church Census will be disappointing for most church leaders, but in the book reporting on the 2002 Census, one Table forecast total attendance ahead for 2005, 2010 and 2020.[16] Although the year 2016 isn't explicitly given, estimating that year from the others (and 1984 and 1994 as well) would give an estimate of 350,000. By that basis, the 2016 figure actually found is 11% higher, almost partly as a result of the numbers of immigrants coming into Scotland, many of whom have joined churches for overseas nationals, but also partly because some young people, not immigrants, choose to attend an ethnic church for a range of reasons.

This is graphed in Figure 2.2, where the future figures for 2016 are not just an extrapolation but also based on life tables since there are so many elderly people in the church in 2016 whose expectation of life is naturally limited.

The black trend line shows the impact of Scottish Pentecostals, immigrants, others who are attending ethnic churches or who are starting new churches for their language group. The rate of decline has clearly lessened even though the line continues to go downwards.

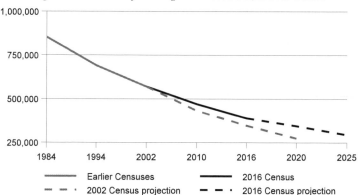

Figure 2.2: Number of churchgoers in Scotland, 1984 to 2025E

Comparison with England

In England, Church Censuses were undertaken in 1989 and 2005, a period 16 years apart (with an extra Census in between in 1998), and over that 16 year period total attendance declined by -2.5% per annum,[17] so the rate of decline experienced over the last few years in Scotland is not dissimilar from recent English church experience. However, in 2016 7.2% of the population of Scotland were attending church on a Sunday, much higher than the 5.3% in England at that time.

The rate of decrease is slowing down

While the numbers going to church are reducing, the *rate* at which they are going down is getting less. Between 1984 and 1994 some 16,300 people (men and women) were leaving the church every year (Table 3.6); between 1994 and 2002 that number was 15,100 and between 2002 and 2016 it was 12,900 per year on average. The smaller rate of decline is partly because more people than expected have joined the church (many immigrants), although also because there are gradually fewer people left to leave.

For example, there are 27 Polish churches in Scotland, all but a few new since 2002. Where are they located? There is one in Dundee, one in Edinburgh, but 25 in Aberdeen (11) or in the Aberdeenshire countryside (14) among the postcodes immediately to the west of Aberdeen, because many Polish labourers are working in the oil industry and the north east of Scotland is where its strength is located. There are also Polish language Masses for congregations in Glasgow. As a consequence the number of churchgoers in 2016 in Aberdeenshire is higher than was expected from the extrapolation made in 2002 of how many it would be in the future. Aberdeenshire in fact has seen the number of its churches increase from 196 in 2002 to 243 in 2016. The change in numbers attending church by Council are shown in Figure 2.3 which shows that Aberdeenshire in fact was the only Council to see growth in the last 14 years.

Figure 2.3: Change in attendance between 2002 and 2016 by Council

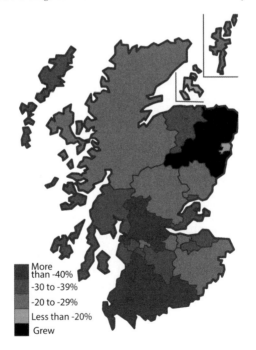

Attendance by Denomination

The total attendance is broken down by denomination as shown in Table 2.4:[18]

Table 2.4: Scottish church attendance by denomination 1984-2025

Denomination	Church of Scotland	Other Presbyterians	Episcopal	Baptist	Independent	Pentecostal	Smaller Denominations	Roman Catholic	Total	% of population
1984	361,340	28,680	20,000	29,240	39,370	5,710¹	23,410	345,950	853,700	*16.9%*
1994	293,170	23,310	20,350	24,530	48,020	9,120	22,900	249,720	691,120	*13.6%*
2002	228,500	26,170	18,870	24,830	41,010	10,090	18,550	202,110	570,130	*11.2%*
% change 02-16	*-40%*	*-32%*	*-29%*	*-28%*	*-25%*	*+87%*	*-1%*	*-33%*	*-32%*	*~*
2016	**136,910**	**17,900**	**13,380**	**17,810**	**30,740**	**18,860**	**18,310**	**135,600**	**389,510**	**7.2%**
2025 E	93,500	16,500	12,600	15,400	24,600	21,400	16,400	94,100	294,500	*5.3%*
1984 % of total	*42*	*3*	*2*	*3*	*5*	*1*	*3*	*41*	*100*	*~*
1994 % of total	*43*	*3*	*3*	*4*	*7*	*1*	*3*	*36*	*100*	*~*
2002 % of total	*40*	*5*	*3*	*4*	*7*	*2*	*3*	*36*	*100*	*~*
2016 % of total	*35*	*5*	*3*	*4*	*8*	*5*	*5*	*35*	*100*	*~*
2025 % of total	*32*	*6*	*4*	*5*	*8*	*7*	*6*	*32*	*100*	*~*

¹ Estimate

This Table shows that Church of Scotland and Roman Catholic church attendances are very similar though as the Church of Scotland has roughly three times as many churches as the Roman Catholics their congregations are necessarily much smaller on average. There are about 20 Roman Catholic congregations in excess of a thousand people, ten times the number in the Church of Scotland. (There are a few such large churches in other denominations also). The then ministers and some members of two prominent churches (New Restalrig and St Catherine's Argyle, both in Edinburgh) left the Church of Scotland in April 2014 as a protest at the 2013 General Assembly vote permitting the ordination of gay clergy, even though doing so meant their ministers having to vacate their manses. Those from New Restalrig formed a new congregation in the Free Church, those from St Catherine's Argyle (the larger church) formed an independent congregation.[19]

The Church of Scotland and the Roman Catholic Church

accounted for four-fifths, 83%, of attendance in 1984, but that proportion had dropped to just over two-thirds, 70%, by 2016. In the interim the proportion of attenders who are in the other denominations or denominational groups in Table 2.2 have all almost doubled, except the Pentecostals who have grown from 1% in 1984 to 5% of the total in 2016.

The Table shows that there has been general decline across most of the denominations since 1984, except for the Pentecostals. The increase in "Other Presbyterians" between 1994 and 2002 is due to the merger of the Congregational Union of Scotland with the United Reformed Church in 2000, their 1994 attendance being included within "Smaller Denominations." The reason for the increase in Independent attendance between 1984 and 1994 is not known, although the Report on the 1994 Census[20] showed that it was mostly an adult increase rather than a child increase, and suggested that it was perhaps because this group tended to focus especially on families thus ensuring two adults from each household.

The Baptists have also declined. The very large majority of Baptist congregations, 92%, belong to the Baptist Union of Scotland who collect details of attendance from their churches every year. In 2015 their total was 18,400 but that included those attending twice, some 1,900 people. So the total figure in 2016 of 17,800 is very close to their figures,[21] the remainder made up of independent Baptist churches, most of whom are very small, apart from Charlotte Chapel which is included here.

The decline in the percentage of the population attending church in Scotland (final column of Table 2.4) is quite severe, especially between 2002 and 2016, but it was in this period that Scotland saw many immigrants, its population increasing by 6.2% in this period from 5.0 million to 5.3 million.

Table 2.1 gives the various constituent denominations or groups within each of the headings used in Table 2.4, but the following Tables give more detail of the three largest composite groups.

Attendance by Other Presbyterians

The other Presbyterians comprise several different Presbyterian groups – the largest is the Free Church of Scotland, followed by (in order of number of churches) the United Free Church of Scotland, the United Reformed Church (included in this group because of its part origins with Presbyterian churches), the Free Church of Scotland (Continuing), the Free Presbyterian Church of Scotland, the Associated Presbyterian Churches, the Reformed Presbyterian Church of Scotland, the International Presbyterian Churches and the Free Presbyterian Church of Ulster. Table 2.5 shows the trend in attendance for the largest of these. Unfortunately the 1984 Census Report[22] did not break down the attendance of "Other Presbyterians" in this detail.

Table 2.5: Sunday Church Attendance in Other Presbyterian Churches

Other Presbyterian denominations	Free Church of Scotland	Free Church of Scot (Con)	United Free Ch of Scotland	Other Presbyterian Ch's	United Reformed Church	Total
1994	<– 15,510 –>		5,840	1,960	~	23,310
2002	12,810	1,520	5,370	2,470	4,000[1]	26,170
2016	**10,210**	**830**	**3,220**	**2,180**	**1,460**	**17,900**
2025	9,400	600	2,300	3,100	1,100	16,500

Scot = Scotland (Con) = (Continuing) Ch's = Churches [1] Estimate

The Free Church of Scotland accounts for over half, 57%, of this group, and in terms of overall Presbyterian church attendance in Scotland it is 7%. It is the Other Presbyterian Churches group which, while only 12% of the total in 2016, are the ones seemingly most likely to grow in the next few years judging by their experience of the last 22 years.

The total Presbyterian church attendance in Scotland shown in Table 2.4 (136,910 + 17,900 = 154,810 people) was 2.9% of the Scottish population in 2016, or one person in every 35, of which the Free Church would be 2, Other Presbyterians would also be 2 and the Church of Scotland the remaining 31.

Attendance by Independent Denominations

There are a large number of independent denominations as the list in Table 2.1 makes clear. Table 2.6 gives the attendance numbers for the main groups (where "Chs" means "Churches").

Table 2.6: Sunday Church Attendance by Independent Denominations

Independent Denominations	Christian Brethren	New Churches	Congregational Chs	Other Churches	Total
1994	17,090	14,340	11,130[1]	5,460	48,020
2002	18,200	12,020	3,580	6,210	40,010
2016	**12,390**	**10,350**	**1,640**	**6,360**	**30,740**
2025	9,800	7,500	800	6,500	24,600

[1] Includes attendance at 54 churches in the Congregational Union of Scotland which joined the United Reformed Church in 2000.

The Open Christian Brethren form the bulk, nine-tenths (88%), of the Brethren numbers, while the remainder are split over many different parties. The term "Open Brethren" is going out of use and the term "Evangelical Church" is now frequently used instead; many of these have a full-time church worker which the old-style Open Brethren often did not.

A number of kind friends helped to get contacts for the Christian Brethren, especially the more exclusive groups. But getting addresses for their churches is difficult and getting replies even when you do get addresses is also very difficult. They have split into many small groups usually over procedural matters. The more strict have a "closed table," admitting only members of their group to communion while "the more liberal meetings do not have a closed Table and so do not produce a list of meetings which is in line with traditional Darbyite teachings."[23]

There are several New Church-like fellowships in Scotland which are included in "New Churches" but the bulk of their attendance is from the groups which have been in existence for over 30 years – Newfrontiers, Vineyard, Jesus Fellowship, c.net and so on. The Congregational Churches, primarily the Congregational Federation (whose churches did not join the United Reformed Church in 2000), are losing numbers more rapidly than other independent churches.

"Other Churches" in this section include the Fellowship of Independent Evangelical Churches which are growing, along with a number of new ones like the Filling Stations – a group of nine fellowships in 2016, all part of the New Wine network.

Attendance in Smaller Denominations

This also is a group which contains many different denominations. "Overseas Nationals" has been split to include the many new churches in Scotland which have been started in recent years, attended by those from China (including three "True Jesus" churches), the Philippines, South Korea, Japan, other Asian countries, Iran, Syria, Poland and elsewhere. "Other Denominations" includes the various Orthodox Churches (few but growing, including their new communities), the Lutheran Churches, Church of the Nazarene, Society of Friends, the Seventh-Day Adventist (relatively small in Scotland), the Grace Communion International, formerly the Worldwide Church of God, with 6 of its 35 UK congregations in Scotland, Local Ecumenical Projects, and a few boarding schools with weekly Sunday assemblies and two military bases where services are regularly held.

Table 2.7: Sunday Church Attendance in the Smaller Denominations

Smaller Denominations	Salvation Army	Methodists	Fresh Expressions	Overseas National Churches	Other Denominations	Total
1994	6,510	6,000	0	3,720[1]	6,670[1]	22,900
2002	5,040	4,040	0	3,880[1]	5,590[1]	18,550
2016	**3,320**	**2,530**	**4,280**	**4,120**	**4,060**	**18,310**
2025	2,000	1,000	6,140	4,260	3,000	16,400

[1] Estimate because Pentecostals have been extracted

Both the Salvation Army and the Methodist Church had about the same number attending church in 1994, but the Methodist Church has lost more people in the last 20 years mainly because the worshippers are older than those attending the Salvation Army Citadels (churches), and it has had to close many churches. Fresh Expressions are a new phenomenon, especially as Messy Church, described above and looked at in more detail later, which is set to grow; it includes Church Without Walls.

"Overseas National Churches" are primarily non-Roman Catholic churches, since the Catholic overseas congregations are included with the Roman Catholic numbers. There are many such congregations, with forms being dispatched to Filipino, Japanese, Korean, Iranian, Chinese, Syrian, Portuguese, Norwegian congregations among others, although we were unable to trace any Protestant Spanish congregation in Scotland. In the Roman Catholic Diocese of Aberdeen there are many Polish congregations but also African, Spanish, French, Syro Malabar, etc.[24]

Gaelic congregations, which are spread throughout Scotland and not just in the Highlands and Eilean Siar, are *not* included in this group but under their appropriate (Presbyterian) denomination.

Pentecostal church attendance

In earlier Censuses the Pentecostals were included as part of "Smaller Denominations" but as explained earlier, have been separated here because of their growth, both in attendance (Table 2.4) and in the number of their churches (Table 2.8). In 1984 the average weekly attendance at a Pentecostal church was estimated at about 100 people; by 2016 this had grown to 110, but is forecast to remain between these two figures in the immediate years ahead.

Pentecostals are mostly Evangelical, 95%, the highest proportion of any denomination apart from the Baptists (99%) and only just more than the Independents (92%). But unlike the Baptists (16%) or Independents (27%), some two-fifths, 41%, of the Pentecostals would classify themselves as Charismatic Evangelical. They are a quarter, 26%, of all the Charismatics in Scotland, slightly less than their proportion in England, 33%.[25]

Like their English counterparts, however, Scottish Pentecostals have been growing rapidly, more than tripling in numbers since 1984, an average rate of growth of +3.8% per annum, a high percentage and double the rate in England, although the numbers being smaller in Scotland are more amenable to a higher percentage.

Why do Pentecostal churches grow? This question was not asked in the Census but Dionne Gravesande, one-time Chair of the (now closed) Afro-Caribbean Evangelical Alliance, speaking to the Global Connections Council,[26] gave the following answers to the question:

- "Mission is more important than justice," she said, acknowledging that some black people are discriminated against by the local government, but put evangelism before getting their rights. This *primacy of mission* has been key in spurring the huge increase in London's Pentecostalism.

- Black Majority Churches are very *relational, and very generous* in their giving. They react to poverty issues, especially on the global scene and readily give money to help. Many travel overseas and see impoverishment first hand, and their whole attitude becomes changed.

- They expect to be given *practical as well as theological teaching* in their church on life style, what the gospel is, how to witness, family life, transmission of the faith to the next generation, the importance of their community, being distinctively different at work, giving stories of changed lives, black history, and so on. They expect much from their pastors and generally pay them well (more than white ministers!).

- They make a huge investment in IT often *using the latest communications* methods and technological resources. (I once visited Kingsway International's 10,000 seater Christian Centre; wherever you sat you could see a screen and hear everything that was being said on the platform).

How many of these reasons apply to Scottish Pentecostals is not known, but their growth against a background of decline is testimony to the fact that these principles certainly work for them! It needs to be put into perspective, however. While in Australia they have also rapidly grown and in 2015 were 3% of the population,[27] in Scotland they were just 0.3% of its population in 2016.

Number of Congregations/Churches

As explained above, although frequently referred to as "churches," the Census is actually based on the number of congregations in a particular denomination. These numbers are given in Table 2.8.

Table 2.8: Numbers of Congregations by Denomination

Denom-ination	Church of Scotland	Other Presbyt-erians	Episcopal	Baptist	Indep-endent	Pente-costal	Smaller Denom-inations	Roman Catholic	Total
1984	1,790	375	306	186	438	58	304	606	4,063
1994	1,691	352	311	203	577	76	356	598	4,164
2002	1,666	392	309	204	509	94	376	594	4,144
2016	**1,502**	**297**	**303**	**185**	**453**	**172**	**301**	**476**	**3,689**
2025	1,432	279	300	179	400	202	295	433	3,520

The total number of congregations in Scotland has been gradually reducing since 1994. In the 22 years since then the number has gone down by 20 a year, a rate which is likely to continue in the years immediately ahead, offset somewhat by the likely increasing number of Pentecostal congregations.

Between 2002 and 2016 the number of congregations in Scotland declined from 4,144 to 3,689, a decline of -11%, or -0.8% per annum. This rate of decline is less than that of attendance decline which means that the average size of a congregation will also have fallen. In 2002 the average Scottish congregation consisted of 138 people, but because the Roman Catholics have such large congregations it is easier for comparative purposes to break this down between Protestants (all the other denominations taken together) and Roman Catholics, for which the average sizes are, respectively, 104 and 340. In 2016 they were, again respectively, 79 and 285, reductions of -25% and -16% respectively on the 2002 figures.

The basic reason why numbers are less is the age profile of congregations, with more people dying or having to cease regular church attendance because they become too frail or need to move into a care home where transport to church is not always available. We look at the age profile in the next chapter.

Smaller congregations presumably mean a depletion in the financial resources available to a church, as well as fewer volunteers to help run community events and church activities. Finding suitable leadership may also become more difficult.

Size of Congregations

It is also possible to analyse the data by the size of a congregation, and compare it with previous Censuses. This is done in Table 2.9:

Table 2.9: Size of Scottish congregations, 1994-2016

Year	Under 10 people	10 to 25	26 to 50	51 to 100	101 to 150	151 to 200	201 to 500	Over 500	Base (=100%)	Average size
1994 % of total	3%[1]	13%[1]	17%	21%	13%[1]	8%[1]	18%[1]	7%[1]	4,164	165
2002 % of total	4%	16%	21%	21%	12%	7%	13%[1]	6%[1]	4,144	140
2016 % of total	**5%**	**19%**	**25%**	**21%**	**10%**	**5%**	**11%**	**4%**	**3,689**	**105**
2016 in figures	184	701	917	775	370	188	406	148	3,689	105

[1] Estimate

It is obvious that the average congregational size is decreasing, as the percentages in each size group diminish with time apart from those for congregations under 50 which increase. Almost half, 49%, of Scottish congregations in 2016 were less than 50 people, and one in 20, 5%, were in single figures. At the other end of the scale the number of congregations over 200 in size has dropped from a quarter of the total, 25%, in 1994 to 15% in 2016.

These vary by denomination as illustrated in Figure 2.10.

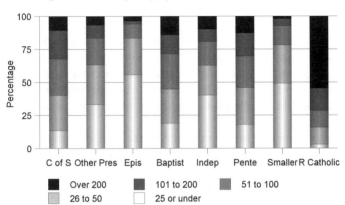

Figure 2.10: Size of congregations by denomination, 2016

This chart shows a number of key features:

- The huge proportion of very small congregations in the Scottish Episcopal Church (56%) and among the various Smaller Denominations (49%), are both more than double the overall percentage across Scotland (24% in Table 2.9).
- The Other Presbyterians and Independent churches also have serious proportions of very small congregations – 33% and 40% respectively. Small congregations are much more likely to become unviable financially, and perhaps struggle with finding able leadership.
- The Church of Scotland, Baptist and Pentecostal churches have a more even balance of proportions of congregations.
- The Roman Catholic Church has more than half its congregations with over 200 people, 55%, each usually requiring several priests to maintain all the services.

The challenges of size, especially declining size, will clearly be real for most denominations. Apart from financial viability, the necessity for adequate leadership, continuing community involvement, as well as having sufficient resources for neighborhood mission all become key issues for the future.

Questions have to be posed on priorities to be followed by individual or groups of congregations, the vision or goals which might be contemplated, and even whether the existing structure within a denomination is adequate for the changed situations of the 21st century.

Opening and Closing Churches

How have these numbers of churches changed since 2002? Table 2.11 indicates approximate numbers opening and closing in this period. It is essentially based on the numbers of churches indicating they had closed in these 14 years when they were initially contacted about the Census. The new churches have come in part from the relevant website or to make the numbers balance.

The various denominations are in most cases groups of denominations, and not all those in any group have had the same opening or closure experience. This is especially true for the Smaller Denominations group which has seen many immigrant churches start and many churches in the older denominations close. Many of the Presbyterian and Roman Catholic closures are sometimes more mergers of congregations than actual closures.

The relatively high number of Baptist closures is almost entirely of Independent Baptist churches, not those within the Baptist Union of Scotland. Likewise some of the churches within the "Other Presbyterian" group are churches which joined it in 2000 forming the United Reformed Church, but many of these former Congregational Churches were small and a few have since closed.

Table 2.11: Numbers of Churches which have
Opened and Closed between 2002 and 2016

Denomination	Church of Scotland	Other Presbyt-erians	Episcopal	Baptist	Indep-endent	Pente-costal	Smaller Denom-inations	Roman Catholic	Total
2002	1,666	392	309	204	509	94	376	594	**4,144**
Opened	13	16	3	5	24	98	141[2]	9	**309**
Closed	-177	-111	-9	-24	-80	-20[1]	-216	-127	**-764**
2016	1,502	297	303	185	453	172	301	476	**3,689**

[1] Estimate [2] Including 82 Messy Churches (Chapter 9)

The figures in Table 2.11 are tentative but they do reflect the new churches started by recent immigrants (within the "Smaller Denominations" group) and by the expanding number of Pentecostal Churches, not all of which succeed (and the closure figure is estimated based on experiences of such churches elsewhere).

Growth or Decline?

One question was added at the last minute to the form – Question 6e "How have the above congregational numbers changed in total over the last 5 years (since 2011)? Have they (a) Increased significantly (over 10%), (b) Increased slightly, (c) Remained fairly static, (d) Decreased somewhat or (e) Decreased significantly?" The answers are shown in Table 2.12:

Table 2.12: Whether Congregational Numbers have
Increased or Decreased since 2011

Increase or decrease	Church of Scotland %	Other Presbyt-erians %	Episcopal %	Baptist %	Indep-endent %	Pente-costal %	Smaller Denom-inations %	Roman Catholic %	**Overall %**
Increased significantly	4	18	8	20	31	36	34	9	*14*
Increased slightly	12	14	15	13	14	18	15	15	*14*
Remained fairly static	26	18	35	24	33	28	16	25	*26*
Decreased somewhat	49	40	32	33	19	17	31	46	*39*
Decreased significantly	9	10	10	10	3	1	4	5	*7*
Base (=100%)	1,502	297	303	185	453	172	301	476	**3,689**

Table 2.12 shows that about a quarter, 26%, of churches had seen their congregations remain more or less static over the last 5 years, while just over a quarter, 28%, had seen them grow, half of these growing significantly since 2011. Almost half, 46%, of congregations had seen decline, 7% of them more than 10%.

If "decreased significantly" was defined as "over 10%", but counting it as -10%, and "decreased somewhat" as a decrease of -5%, with "increased slightly" as +5% and "increased significantly" as +10%, then the average of the above overall percentages is -0.55%, which over the 14 years 2002 to 2016 is an average decline of -2.4% per annum, very close to the actual measured -2.7% per annum mentioned earlier. This suggests the rates of decline given by the churches are close to reality.

It is the Independent, Pentecostal and Smaller Denominations which have seen the largest proportions of growing congregations, all averaging close to 50% (total of the two "increased" lines). Why did these denominational groups grow? Table 2.11 shows that a main reason was because they started new congregations – in that table these three groups had the largest numbers of new congregations. This is not necessarily the whole story but it is a significant factor in it.

The other denominations all saw more than two-fifths of their congregations decline, and the Church of Scotland almost three-fifths, 58%. Merging congregations may help in the problem of pastoral oversight with a smaller number of ministers, but it doesn't suggest that this is a formula to facilitate growth.

The percentage of churches reporting they had increased significantly in Argyll and Bute, Edinburgh City and Falkirk were all about double the overall average.

People are also joining

The figures in Table 2.4 are *net* figures, that is, they are the results of those joining less those leaving. How many are joining? Table 2.11 shows that at least 309 churches have started between 2002 and 2016, but a new church will have initially a smaller congregation than an established church. Table 2.9 shows the size of a congregation in 2016 is 105 people; suppose a new church is half that number. New churches usually attract new people from outside the existing church, though there will be a nucleus of existing church people to help start the new congregation. Suppose the Messy Church church percentage of 25% existing church people applies. Then the number of new people joining churches in Scotland between 2002 and 2016 is over 12,000 people.

Question 6e asked if a church's congregation had changed significantly (that is by at least 10%) since 2011, and 14% of churches answered positively. Working this through for each denominational group according to the size of their churches shows that about 6,000 people have joined their churches in these 14 years. Table 3.1 indicates also that there are at least 52,000 children in church in 2016 who were not born in 2002.

So we have a total decline of 250,000 church people between 2002 and 2016, offset by over 300 new churches starting bringing in 12,000 new people, growth of some existing congregations by 6,000 people, and 52,000 new children, resulting in an overall decline of 180,000 (570,000 in 2002 reducing to 390,000 in 2016).

Services not every Sunday

Some 5%, one in every 20, of Scottish churches do not have a weekly service on a Sunday. Of these

- 1% hold services on a weekday instead
- 1% hold services every fortnight
- 3% hold services monthly (especially in some Scottish Episcopal, Independent, Presbyterian and Smaller Denominations' churches)
- ½% hold services less frequently than once a month.

The first three groups were all included in the Census, but the attendance at the small number of churches holding fairly infrequent services, often in outlying areas, especially in the Highlands, were not included in the overall figures – in total these would amount to perhaps 2,000 people. For churches holding services on weekdays, Saturday was the most popular alternative, followed equally by Tuesdays, Wednesdays or Thursdays.

Several Services every Sunday

The number of services held on a Sunday varied by denomination as shown in Table 2.13.

Table 2.13: Number of services held most Sundays, by denomination, 2016

Number of services held on a Sunday	Church of Scotland %	Other Presbyt- erians %	Episcopal %	Baptist %	Indep- endent %	Pente- costal %	Smaller Denom- inations %	Roman Catholic %	**Overall %**
Normally only one	81	48	70	49	38	69	84	42	**67**
Two	17	45	20	46	34	21	13	21	**24**
Three or four	2	6	9	5	27	10	2	28	**8**
Five or more	0	1	1	0	1	0	1	9	**1**
Base (=100%)	1,502	297	303	185	453	172	301	476	**3,689**
Average number	1.2	1.7	1.5	1.6	2.1	1.5	1.2	2.4	**1.5**

Two-thirds, 67%, of churches held just one service on a Sunday, although there were sometimes extra Sunday services once a month or extra evening services, or additional services for special language groups (such as Polish Masses) as necessary and opportunity allowed. A quarter, 24%, held two services, and the remainder three or more.

Roman Catholics held the most services (Masses) on a Sunday, followed by Independent Churches, many of which continued the traditional morning and evening pattern. Many Other Presbyterian (52%) and Baptist (51%) Churches continued that same pattern. It was the larger churches which tended to have three or more services (for all except the Roman Catholics this was nearly always three). A small number of non-Roman Catholic churches said they held five or more.

Of the 9% Roman Catholic Churches holding 5 or more Masses on a Sunday, half were just five and the other half were more – eight or nine perhaps.

Attending more than one service

If there was more than one service on a Sunday, how many in the congregation attended more than one service? This varied as shown in Table 2.14:

*Table 2.14: Percentage of adults attending more
than one service on a Sunday*

Percentage attending more than one service on a Sunday	Church of Scotland %	Other Presbyt-erians %	Episc-opal %	Baptist %	Indep-endent %	Pente-costal %	Smaller Denom-inations %	Roman Catholic %	**Overall %**
Attending 2 or more services	4	39	5	25	32	18	6	2	**9**

Overall, 9% of those attending church went twice on a Sunday, so that if one was counting attend*ances* and not attend*ers* it would add an additional 35,000 people (0.6% of the population) coming on a Sunday, or a grand total of 425,000 people attending at least one service.

Of these the Other Presbyterian (39%), Independent (32%) and Baptist (25%) Churches were most likely to have multiple attendances, followed by the Pentecostals (18%). The other denominations collectively accounted for just 4% of those attending.

The percentage attending two or more services varied by Council. Eilean Siar had by far the highest percentage with no less than 41% of their churchgoers going twice or more on a Sunday. This was followed by Falkirk with 22%, East Renfrewshire and Highland with 17% each, and Dundee City and Stirling with 15% each. One tenth, 10%, of those in both the Orkney and Shetland Islands attended twice also.

So what does all this say?

This chapter has looked at the basic number of existing congregations (rather than churches) in Scotland in 2016, and has explicitly included one group of smaller charismatic denominations as the Pentecostals for the first time as they are rapidly growing (previously within "Smaller Denominations").

The basic number of worshipers has shrunk substantially since the last Census in 2002, but at about the same rate as congregations are declining in Britain as a whole, and not quite as fast as expected because of the growth of the charismatic and immigrant churches (as also in England). The decline is especially great in the Church of Scotland whose numbers have declined -40% between 2002 and 2016, faster than any other group of churches. A few individual denominations have seen an even sharper decline in this period (like the Free Church of Scotland (Continuing), United Reformed Church, and the Congregational Federation).

The Pentecostal growth is important even though it does not compensate for decline elsewhere. It would seem that their prioritising of evangelism has been the key to their expansion, as well as the practical teaching given in applying Christian theology to everyday life and circumstance.

While the number of congregations has reduced, this needs to be put in the context of some 310 new congregations started in the last 14 years. Although reality may not have quite met expectations, many congregations (14%, one in seven) say they have experienced significant growth in the last five years, although two fifths (39%) recognize they have "decreased somewhat."

The numbers are the result of new people joining less those who have left. The numbers joining are estimates, but suggest that whilst there are 180,000 fewer people in church in Scotland in 2016 than in 2002, that is offset by almost 18,000 new people not in church previously. (The next chapter also shows that at least 52,000 children in church in 2016 have been born since 2002).

A few churches hold services mid-week or less frequently than every week, while some regularly average more than two services on a Sunday (especially Roman Catholic and Independent Churches). Some 9% of worshipers attend twice on a Sunday, a practice seen especially in the Other Presbyterian and Independent Churches many of which maintain a regular morning and evening service. In Eilean Siar (the Western Isles) two-fifths (41%) of worshippers attended twice every Sunday.

Congregations generally have become smaller, however, since 2002, which obviously means more smaller congregations (25 or under) and fewer large ones (200 or over). A third of congregations, 33%, had 50 or fewer in 1984, but in 2016 that had grown to virtually half (49%), with the resulting strain of viability and leadership which often follows. Likewise the percentage of churches with over 200 on a Sunday has reduced from 25% in 1984 to 15% in 2016, with almost half (47%) of these being Roman Catholic Churches.

It is the Scottish Episcopal Church and the various Smaller Denominations which are most likely to have smaller congregations (both about half their total are 25 or under), but Independent Churches and Other Presbyterians also have many (40% and 33% respectively). The challenges of reducing size are of key importance for the years ahead.

3

THE AGE OF SCOTTISH CHURCHGOERS

While the total number of churchgoers is a critical finding in any Church Census, breaking that down by the simple demographic factors of age and gender is also significant since, especially with several measurements over time, the trend in them gives a valuable insight into the broad overall situation. In this Census the question of age and gender was completed in detail by a large majority of churches, including some of the very largest with congregations of 500 or more.

In order to obtain precise information on age and gender, and also on ethnicity, distance lived from the church, length of time attending that congregation, and frequency of attendance, "slips" of paper, or mini-forms, were made available to minsters or administrators for photocopying and giving out to the congregation for individual completion. The answers could then be added to give the totals put on the actual Census form.

Age and Gender of Churchgoers

The proportions attending on the given Sunday on the Census form are as shown in Table 3.1, and illustrated in Figure 3.2:

Table 3.1: Age and gender of Scottish Churchgoers, 2016

Age-group	4 and under	5 to 11	12 to 15	16 to 24	25 to 34	35 to 44	45 to 54	55 to 64	65 to 74	75 to 84	85 & over	TOTAL
Men	7,100	13,160	5,810	7,430	10,710	12,900	16,290	21,610	30,920	22,030	6,730	**154,690**
Women	8,180	15,900	6,150	9,400	13,740	18,330	23,590	34,250	52,770	40,230	12,280	**234,820**
TOTAL	**15,280**	**29,060**	**11,960**	**16,830**	**24,450**	**31,230**	**39,880**	**55,860**	**83,690**	**62,260**	**19,010**	**389,510**
As percentages												
Men	*1.8*	*3.4*	*1.5*	*1.9*	*2.8*	*3.3*	*4.2*	*5.5*	*7.9*	*5.7*	*1.7*	***39.7***
Women	*2.1*	*4.1*	*1.6*	*2.4*	*3.5*	*4.7*	*6.0*	*8.8*	*13.6*	*10.3*	*3.2*	***60.3***
TOTAL	***3.9***	***7.5***	***3.1***	***4.3***	***6.3***	***8.0***	***10.2***	***14.3***	***21.5***	***16.0***	***4.9***	***100***
Population	*5.4*	*7.5*	*2.6*	*11.2*	*13.0*	*12.5*	*14.8*	*12.8*	*10.3*	*6.1*	*2.3*	*100*

Figure 3.2: Age of Churchgoers compared with General Population, 2016

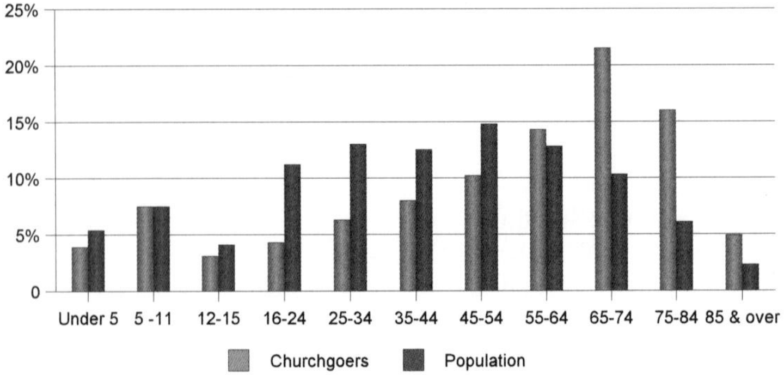

The bar-chart illustrates very clearly that the church has proportionately far fewer people aged especially between 16 and 54 and far more aged 65 and over compared with the general population. The chart also shows that there are less children under 5 in church (but perhaps they were in the creche?), and less aged 12 to 15 but the differences here in both of these groups are relatively small. The largest differences are with those aged 65 to 84, this age range accounting for almost two-fifths, 38%, of all churchgoers but only 16% of the population.

Table 3.1 also shows that the proportion of men in church in 2016 in Scotland was 40% of the total against 60% of women, while the population proportions were respectively 49% and 51%.[28] Figure 3.3 illustrates how this gender proportion varies by age.

Figure 3.3: Gender proportions of Scottish Churchgoers in 2016 by age

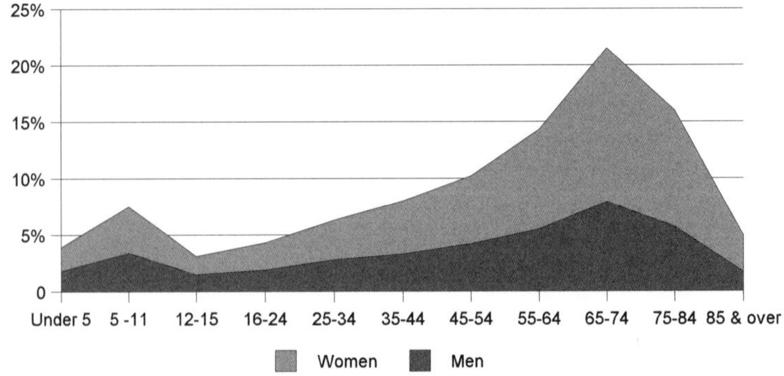

The proportion of men in the Scottish churches has been growing. In 1984 37% of churchgoers were male, in 1994 the proportion was 39% and in 2002 it was 40%, the same as in 2016. However, the difference in numbers between men and women is especially marked after the age of 55 to 64. There are almost twice as many women as men attending Scottish churches aged 65 to 74 and while it is true that women live longer than men and thus more women can be expected at older ages, this proportion is much greater than normal demographic differences. In the general population of Scotland in 2016 there were 1.25 women for every man aged 65 or over; in the churches the proportion was 1.76!

In terms of people available for helping with community work, having so many older people, the large majority of whom will have retired, is an advantage as many of these will still have reasonable amounts of energy and health. But this poses obvious problems for the future, for those who are 65 to 74 today will be 75 to 84 in 10 years' time, and will have less energy and probably more ill health.

There is also the difficulty in outreach. While older people are often the backbone of the church, the image of "an old people's club" may deter younger people from joining. The relatively large number of Messy Churches has already been mentioned, but perhaps one reason for their popularity is that they tend to appeal to younger people, especially families with small children.

There is more or less parity of numbers between men and women up to about the age of 35, although women outnumber men slightly in every age-group. However, Figure 3.3 shows the large drop in numbers of younger teenagers, often called "tweenagers", between ages 12 and 15, something which is not unique to Scotland but which is happening in England as well, although in England the number of young men aged 15 to 19 in 2005 was slightly greater than the number of young women in church of that age-group.

Trends in Age over Time

The age-bands given in Table 3.1 were not the ones used in previous Scottish Church Censuses. The Planning Committee, however, felt it was important that comparisons be made with data collected previously which means reformulating the data in Table 3.1 to fit the age-bands used previously, and Table 3.4 is the result. Having several years of data allows an estimate to be made for 2025. The table is illustrated in Figure 3.5.

Table 3.4: Age of Scottish Churchgoers using the age-bands of previous Censuses

Men	Under 15	15 to 19	20 to 29	30 to 44	45 to 64	65 & over	Total
1984	93,910	17,070	25,610	42,690	76,830	59,760	315,870
1994	60,200	15,820	20,740	41,470	69,110	62,200	269,540
2002	43,610	11,400	17,100	30,510	62,710	60,720	226,050
% change	-44%	-58%	-45%	-40%	-40%	-2%	-32%
2016	**24,620**	**4,750**	**9,480**	**18,260**	**37,900**	**59,680**	**154,690**
2025	15,510	3,210	5,390	14,140	29,340	49,910	117,500
Women	Under 15	15 to 19	20 to 29	30 to 44	45 to 64	65 & over	Total
1984	119,520	25,610	51,220	85,370	128,060	128,050	537,830
1994	64,200	18,740	34,550	76,020	117,490	110,580	421,580
2002	54,810	12,400	19,610	50,310	93,930	113,020	344,080
% change	-48%	-54%	-38%	-50%	-38%	-7%	-32%
2016	**28,690**	**5,720**	**12,090**	**25,200**	**57,840**	**105,280**	**234,820**
2025	19,470	4,110	8,270	15,980	40,420	88,750	177,000
Percentage of Men + Women combined in total							
1984	25	5	9	15	24	22	100
1994	18	5	8	17	27	25	100
2002	17	4	6	14	28	31	100
2016	**14**	**3**	**5**	**11**	**25**	**42**	**100**
2025	12	2	5	10	24	47	100

The scales in the two charts in Figure 3.5 are deliberately the same and show a very similar picture – one of huge decline in the numbers attending church in Scotland, and across all ages except those 65 and over, a picture which is not dissimilar to English churchgoers, except that those aged 45 to 64 do not decrease quite so rapidly. The implications of these graphs are serious – should the extrapolation to 2025 prove more or less correct, then almost half the churchgoers then remaining in Scotland will be 65 or over.

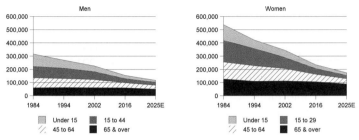

Figure 3.5: Age-groups of Scottish Churchgoers, 1984 to 2025E

The two lines in Table 3.4 labelled "% change" show the percentage drop in that particular age-group in numbers between 2002 and 2016. For both men and women the largest percentage drop was for the older teenagers, between 15 and 19. Women also had a high percentage drop for both those under 15 and those aged 30 to 44 (many of the latter will probably be mothers). These Scottish percentages of female decline are at a greater rate than is occurring in England, but this is probably because of the impact of the high number of immigrants in England.

It is obvious that those 65 and over are hardly declining at all – a -2% drop for men and a -7% drop for women over a period of 14 years is very small. In these 14 years many churchgoers will have died, but their numbers have been replaced by those in their 50s and early 60s. In the years ahead there are not sufficient numbers in their 40s and 50s to replace those moving into their 60s.

The overall proportion of men in 2016 is 40%, but this varies from 46% for those under 15, 45% for those 15 to 19, 44% for those in their 20s, 42% for those aged 30 to 44, 40% for those 45 to 64 and 36% for those aged 65 or over. This reflects normal male mortality, as well as those 65 or over being 42% of total attenders.

It should be noted that the change in numbers in Table 3.4 are net numbers, that is to say, while it shows people leaving the church, that number is made up of people joining the church less those leaving the church. Why do people leave a church? The most common reasons are, quoting English figures for the Church of England and the Christian Brethren:[29]

- The ministry no longer seems relevant to them (or their children) (so said 15% Anglicans in 2015 and 28% Brethren in 2013)
- People move to another area (so 30% Anglicans, 32% Brethren)
- Death (so 42% Anglicans, 28% Brethren)
- Moving into residential care
- Having moved, people are unable to find a suitable church so stop going
- Lost their commitment or interest (13% Anglican, 12% Brethren).

It is the last two which especially have pastoral concerns. How can one help those who are moving home to find a suitable church at the same time?

Losing 10 congregations per month

The overall picture, however, is confused somewhat because the different Censuses have taken place at unequal intervals of time. Table A1 in the Appendix therefore shows the changing of the numbers but averaged at a per annum rate between them, and this Table is depicted in Figure 3.6.

This chart shows, as already mentioned, that the per annum rate of decline has been reducing since 1994 for both men and women, and for women since 1984, but the present loss of 13,000 people a year in 2016 is equivalent to 124 congregations closing per annum, or 10 churches every month. Starting new or replacement churches or congregations is therefore vitally important, especially in some of the rural areas where closures have been highest.

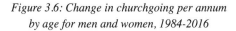

*Figure 3.6: Change in churchgoing per annum
by age for men and women, 1984-2016*

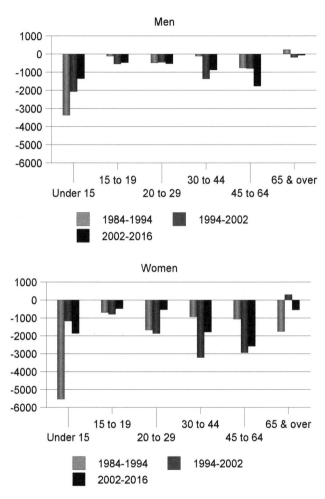

Figure 3.6 also indicates that especially high numbers of some age-groups have left at particular times. For example, the period 1984 to 2002 saw many women in their 20s leave, and the period 1994 to 2002 saw many men and women leave aged 30 to 44, many of whom probably will have been couples with families, and so are likely to have taken their children with them. The

latest period 2002 to 2016 has seen a heavy loss of men and women aged 45 to 64, some of whom are likely to have been leaders or helpers working with various church community activities.

Figure 3.7 shows the number of people by age-group by gender attending church in Scotland for the years 1984 and 2016.

Figure 3.7: Scottish churchgoers by gender, 1984 and 2016

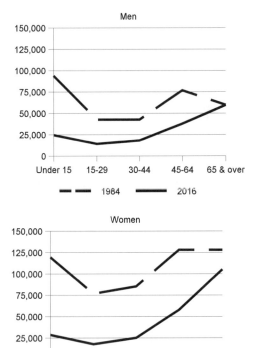

These graphs show that more women attend church than men. Is this because women are more religious than men, or just that they feel more comfortable with expressing it and more under the necessity to express it, particularly in terms of churchgoing?

Figure 3.6 also shows that far more women have stopped going to church between 1984 and 2016 than men. The two graphs also show that the drop among the numbers who are 65 and over is either virtually zero for men or the smallest of all age group differences for women. Why are the women especially leaving the church?

The American Barna Group has researched women and the church, and has found in fact that women in 2015 were less likely to attend church regularly than men, a reverse of the situation 10 years earlier. They sought to ascertain why this was so, and found several reasons for American women,[30] some of which may be relevant to Scottish women:

- Women are putting churchgoing at a *lower priority* than before, with family and work coming first very often (but not a commitment to furthering their career).
- They were just busy, really, *really busy*. 72% of women felt stressed out, 58% felt tired, and 48% said they were overcommitted.
- *Changing family structures*. Women are getting married later now, starting families later, preferring to become financially stable before embarking on marriage.

This scenario is less likely to be true of older women attending church where the above factors are probably less relevant, though for Third Agers other factors come into play. In some parts of Scotland, especially in the Highlands, official church teaching discourages women being ordained as leaders; could this be one reason why women are leaving the church?

Some Scottish churches are negative about divorcees or unmarried mothers, and, as elsewhere, Scotland has many women in both categories. Women in these situations feel defensive and disapproved of, so drop out. Scotland also has a long history of Sunday trading, and many women are forced to work on Sundays (there is no opt-out as elsewhere).

On the other hand, some unpublished research of a small study undertaken in the aftermath of the 1984 Census found that some women were expected to go to church to *represent* their family, so the rest didn't need to go!

Age by Denomination

In order to evaluate better the variation of the age of churchgoers by denomination we can return to the detailed age-groups in which the 2016 data was collected. The detail is given in Table 3.8:

Table 3.8: Age of Scottish churchgoers by denomination, 2016

Age-group %	Church of Scotland %	Other Presbyt-erians %	Episcopal %	Baptist %	Indep-endent %	Pente-costal %	Smaller Denom-inations %	Roman Catholic %	Overall %
Under 5	3	4	3	5	4	7	7	4	**4**
5 to 11	6	8	5	9	9	10	13	8	**8**
12 to 15	2	4	2	4	6	5	4	4	**3**
16 to 24	2	5	4	7	8	9	9	6	**4**
25 to 34	3	6	6	7	10	13	10	10	**6**
35 to 44	5	8	8	10	10	13	11	13	**8**
45 to 54	8	11	9	15	12	17	11	12	**10**
55 to 64	15	14	16	15	13	13	10	14	**14**
65 to 74	27	20	25	16	15	8	13	17	**22**
75 to 84	22	16	17	10	10	4	9	9	**16**
85 and over	7	4	5	2	3	1	3	3	**5**
Base (=100%)	136,910	17,900	13,380	17,810	30,740	18,860	18,310	135,600	**389,510**
Average age	60	52	56	46	45	39	42	47	**53**

The denominations fall into three groups, defined by their average age:

- The youngest – the Pentecostals and the Smaller Denominations, both of which have between a fifth and a quarter of their attenders under 16, 22% and 24% respectively, and consequently have a smaller percentage 65 or over than any other group – 13% and 25% respectively, the latter partly because Smaller Denominations include the Methodists and Church of the Nazarene which are small but relatively elderly.
- The "middle-aged", with their average age between 45 and 47, the Independents, Baptists and Roman Catholics. These three have between 16% and 19% of attenders who are under 16, and 28% or 29% who are 65 or over.
- The "elderly" with an average age of over 50 – the Other Presbyterians, the Scottish Episcopal Church and the Church of Scotland (whose average age is 60). These have between 10% and 16% who are under 16, and 40% to 56% who are 65 and over.

The difference between those attending the churches in these three groups is quite signifcant. The Church of Scotland, for example, has one of the highest age profiles of any denomination in the UK; in the English Census in 2005 those with the highest average ages, both of 55, were the Methodists and the United Reformed Church.[31] The difference between the above three groupings, taking a weighted average of their various percentages, is shown in Figure 3.9.

Figure 3.9 shows that the key difference is less the percentage of attenders who are 85 and over but much more the percentage who are aged 65 to 74. All three groups have a reasonable percentage aged 5 to 11, and a significant drop among those aged 12 to 15, but it is the older people who create the greatest differences.

Figure 3.9: Percentage of churchgoers in three groups of denominations, 2016

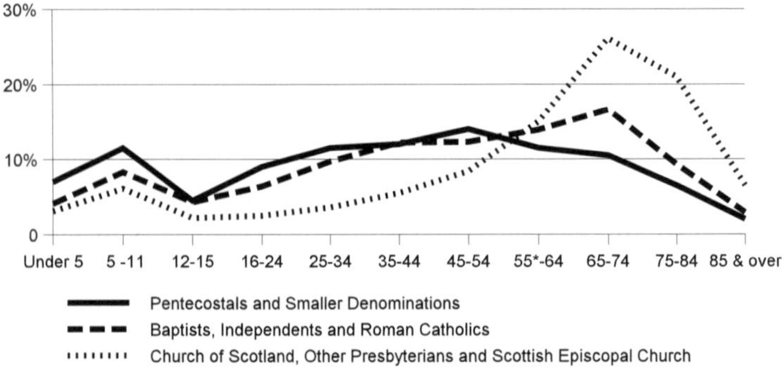

Children in a Creche

Over 50,000 children joined Scottish churches during the years 2002 to 2016. Most churches who have children attending include them in their Sunday morning congregation for at least part of the time, but some have no children who come in to the service at all. Many of these will be in a creche for the very young, who usually will not come into the service. One question on the form asked how many children were in this category.

Two-thirds, 69%, of churches had some children attending who did not come into the service. These children accounted for 7.5% of all children coming to church, just over 4,200 children in total, and just over a quarter of all those aged 4 and under (from Table 3.1),which suggests that most, if not all, are babies or toddlers in a creche.

Generational Differences

There are large generational differences in many societal factors of life. It may be helpful to quote some of these in order to help church leaders consider how best each generation may be reached with the Gospel. There is a very large difference, for example, in the expectations and values that many Gen Yers (those born between 1983 and 2001) have from the outlook of those likely to be their managers (Gen Xers, those born between 1964 and 1982) or their employers (Boomers, those born 1945 to 63). An article in *Professional Manager* three years ago summarised the differences very neatly for three generations:[32]

Table 3.10: Differences between generations

Topic	Gen Y	Gen X	Boomers
Year born	1983-2001	1964-1982	1945-1963
Lives	In a shared house with friends, or a rented flat with partner	In family home; children might be any age from toddlers to teenagers	In family home with partner; children have grown up and moved out or (for the less fortunate) boomeranged home. Owns his home outright, but is lender of first resort to his highly mortgaged Xer children.
Workplace attire	Casual clothing, including jeans and sneakers, for meetings and day-to-day work	Suit and tie for client meetings; suit and no tie, or smart separates, for day-to-day work	Suit and tie
Accessories	iPad	Smartphone	Wristwatch, Blackberry
Works best	On collaborative projects, given encouragement, training and mentoring	Given freedom to choose the best process to reach the desired result	In teams, given strong direction on tasks
Leadership style	Sociable, consultative, unassuming, optimistic	Informal and hands-off; results-focussed, with high expectations	Supportive, hands-on, but with clear delineation between manager and team
Loyalty to employer	Low; not career-focussed, but likes to build a network of professional contacts to ensure any career move will be to an interesting and rewarding role	Moderate; works hard, but has no qualms about changing jobs to climb the career ladder	High; willing to make sacrifices for the good of the company
Water-cooler conversation	Anything and everything, including personal life and plans to change career	Changes with the business, holidays, kids, home improvement, the 1990s	Sport, politics, television, grandchildren, the 1960s
Likes	Communicating via Twitter and text, multitasking, frequent rewards and recognition, active focus on professional development	Deserved rewards, efficient systems, regular feedback, communicating by email or telephone	Face-to-face communication, respect for authority, dedication to work, enthusiasm
Dislikes	Scepticism, condescension, lack of clear instructions, feeling an employer does not share beliefs and priorities	Micro management, focus on process rather than results, gimmicky training and incentive programmes, laziness, distraction	Workplace conflict, competition, overly bureaucratic or disinterested managers

Changes across the years

To put all these changes into perspective, Figure 3.11 gives the numbers attending Scottish churches on an average Sunday for the four Censuses, with the projection for 2025 given in Table 3.4 also shown. The years also give the proportion of the population attending.

This bar chart shows the enormity of the challenge facing Scottish church leaders. If present trends continue until 2025, then there will be almost as many people 65 and over in the church as collectively under 65, with obvious concerns over viability, energy to run church and community events, frailty, leadership, as well as coping with many funerals.

Figure 3.11: Sunday Church Attendance by age, 1984 to 2025E

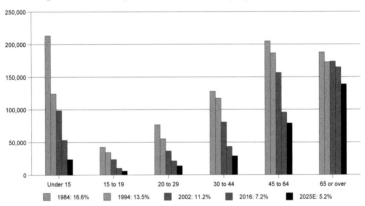

The various years in which Scottish Church Censuses were undertaken were those when it was most convenient to do so and were not planned decades in advance. Likewise the age-groups used have been those convenient for each Census. This means, however, that comparing change from one time period to another, or from one age-group to another, becomes awkward because the intervals between each vary.

An attempt to remedy this is given in Table A2a in the Appendix, which has been constructed by taking the numbers in each age-group attending in each Census and estimating them through linear regression to give figures for each year ending in "0" from 1980 to 2030, and the age-groups into revised age-groups each of just 10 years. This has the advantage of tracing how many, say, teenagers (10 to 19 year olds) going to church in 2000 are still in church when they have reached their 20s in 2010. The table looks complicated, but an explanation is given with it in the Appendix on how to read it. In particular, it shows very clearly what is already known, that the greatest fall-out of those attending church are younger people. Once the habit of churchgoing is established in a person's life they tend to keep on going if they can.

The Table is also useful in that it breaks down the older group into its constituent years of those aged between 60 and 69, 70 and 79, and 80 and over, from which may be estimated numbers attending in the age-groups used in the 2016 Census for those 65 and over.

Older people in church

Older people are senior to the groups mentioned by the names of Gen Y, Gen X and Boomers. If they need an appellation they are called the "Seniors", born 1944 or earlier. Many will have memories of WWII and will have formed their life values in the 1930s. The term "Third Age" has been employed by the Office for National Statistics for those aged between 65 and 74, and the age range for "Fourth Age" and "Fifth Age" derive from it. The concern for current church leaders must surely be in the proportions of churchgoers in the 65 and older age-group and the likely increase in those proportions in the years ahead. Table 3.12 reflects some of the social and church differences of these older people, and Table 3.13 which follows gives the numbers in these older groups actually attending church in Scotland and how they have changed since 1984 and might continue to change by 2025.

Table 3.12: Factors about the elderly

Age-group	Name	Activity	Sufficiency	Church life	Sense of belonging to a church [33]	% who went to Sunday School [34]
55 to 64	~	Still employed	Earning a salary	In leadership	43%	30%
65 to 74	Third Age	Retired	Travelling with Saga?	Supporting role	34%	33%
75 to 84	Fourth Age	Grand-parenting	Loss of spouse	May need help to get to church	28%	43%
85 & over	Fifth Age	Confined to home	Increasing dependency	Only attend on special occasions	19%	49%

Table 3.13: Estimated number of Scottish churchgoers,
65 and over, 1980 to 2030

Year	65 - 74	75-84	85 & over	**Total 65 & over**	Average age	% of all attenders
1980	96,700	76,820	16,750	**190,270**	76.0	21%
1990	88,990	71,830	18,980	**179,800**	76.3	24%
2000	82,600	69,820	21,540	**173,960**	76.7	28%
2010	81,850	64,890	22,330	**169,070**	76.7	36%
2020	75,580	58,060	20,390	**154,030**	76.7	44%
2030	60,700	50,110	18,600	**129,410**	77.0	55%

The trend in the last two columns is very similar to the trend across the same age-groups for English churchgoers,[35] so the ageing problems church leaders face in both England and Scotland are comparable. In both countries, over the next 10 years or so, almost half of all churchgoers will be 65 or over, and probably over half by 2025. While, of course, older people are an essential part of the church the difficulty comes in how best to provide both for them and for those who are younger.

There are a number of implications from the figures in this Table:

- The *retirement* age of leaders – should that be increased? Roman Catholic priests already have a retirement age of 75. The average age of a Scottish minister in 2016 was 57 [see Table 7.2] and if he or she retires at, say, 70 instead of 65, then by the time they come to retire, in say 2030, over half of their congregation could be over 65, if the percentages in Table 3.13 turn out to be about correct. Older leaders would minister to older congregations, but they would not necessarily attract younger people.

- The *impact* of older people – not all are *physically* able to manage stairs, for example. Not all older people like loud music in their worship. Should churches able to afford such appoint a supplementary Minister for Older People? A few worshippers will become centenarians. The increased life expectancy among men is also likely to mean more older married couples with great-grandchildren.

- How does one best help and encourage older people with *grandchildren*, great-grandchildren and even great-great-grandchildren? In what practical ways can Christian grandparents build into their roles as child-minders in sharing Christian truth and values? Child minding is sharing the Christian truth and values of love, understanding, patience, joy, time, interest, prayer, talking about Jesus, Bible stories, etc. Pre-school years are the most formative of all.

- *Finance*: People aged between 50 and 74 spent twice as much as the under-30s on cinema tickets between 2000 and 2010. Their restaurant spending also increased by 33% while the under-30s spent 18% less.[36] While these are facts from the general population, Third Age churchgoers are not immune from current trends, although it may not necessarily apply across all denominations. Third Agers may be very committed, but may become less able to support their church as much as perhaps they used to when earning a salary.

- *Driving* is the most common form of transport for older people in the UK, with 68% of households where someone is aged 70+ having their own car.[37] Giving up driving is more likely to be because of declining health, rather than advancing age as such. However, the older people get, the less easy it is for them to travel to church, doctor or hospital. Can churches help by providing some kind of transport rota, even "mini-bussing" people to church?

- While the proportion of elderly people in church may be increasing there are still many thousands *who do not come* to church, who still need to hear the Gospel and find the Saviour. How can those outside the church be more effectively evangelized? Should part of ministerial training be devoted to the concerns for reaching the elderly? How help older people reach out to others in their generation?

- Some of these will be people who used to attend church but for whatever reason *have dropped out* and form part of what is sometimes called the "invisible church." It is interesting that Church Army research has shown that a third, 35%, of those attending Fresh Expressions/Messy Church are those who used to attend but have started to attend again, feeling this group is now "their" church.[38] On average they will have been out of church for about 8 or 10 years,[39] although the more recent 2013 research by Dr Steve Aisthorpe in Scotland suggests it may be longer (perhaps 14 years on average).[40]

- If so many older people are in the church, the *image* of the church can easily resemble an Old People's Club, a sort of special U3A group.[41] Younger people need to be reached with the Gospel also, and to feel an appreciated and integral part of God's people. A mutual "adopting" of an older person by a younger, and vice-versa, can sometimes lead to a very fruitful, caring relationship.

Age of churchgoer by size of congregation

Are churchgoers of different ages spread uniformly across different sized congregations? The answer is NO, they are not, as the graph in Figure 3.14 makes clear.

Figure 3.14: Age of churchgoers by size of Scottish congregation, 2016

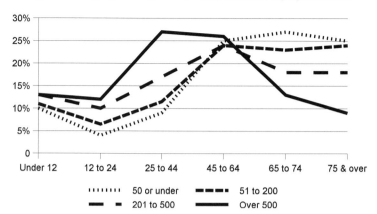

The graph shows that the larger a church the greater the percentage of those aged 12 to 24 and 25 to 44 attending. While the percentage of those aged 45 to 64 is much the same whatever the size of the church, the larger the church the smaller the percentage of those aged 65 to 74 and 75 and over attending.

It also shows that those aged 12 to 24 and especially those aged 25 to 44 are much more likely to attend larger churches, something also true in English churches, and probably more widely still. Just 4% of congregations with under 51 people attending are aged 12 to 24, and 9% are aged 25 to 44, compared with 12% and 27% respectively for congregations of 500 or over.

The average age of a congregation with 25 or fewer people is 61, while the average age in a congregation of over 500 is 43 (shown in the final column of Table A7).

This simply identifies two related situations – the paucity of those likely to be parents of young children (and who would probably have the energy and maybe the time to volunteer for helping with church activities like the Sunday School) in smaller congregations, and the fact that the larger churches, having such personnel resources, are therefore likely to attract younger families.

So what does all this say?

This chapter has looked at the age and gender of those going to church in Scotland. There are more women who go than men – three women for every two men, but over the 32 years between the first and fourth Church Censuses twice as many women have left the church as men, 300,000 to 160,000.

There is a smaller proportion of churchgoers than in the population generally for all ages up to 54, but thereafter the percentage of churchgoers exceeds the percentage in the population in each age-group. The difference is especially pronounced for those between 64 and 84, 19% of churchgoers to 9% population. There is an especially large number of churchgoing women aged 65 to 74.

Numbers are decreasing in each age-group, with teenagers of both genders (15 to 19) decreasing most and also women aged 30 to 44. Overall numbers are equivalent to losing 10 congregations every month. The Presbyterian Denominations and the Scottish Episcopal Church have the oldest congregations and the Pentecostals and the Smaller Denominations the youngest. The generational differences are considerable.

It is the older churchgoers which in a sense cause the greatest concern, not in terms of their attendance but their ageing. There were 190,000 men and women 65 or over attending church in 1980 but, if the present rate of decline continues, there will be only 120,000 by 2030, an overall decline of 1% per annum, but likely to double in the 2020s. By 2030 those 65 and above could be over half of all churchgoers. Such a preponderance of older people has many implications for the church as it faces the future, not least that their demise is not being replaced by younger people.

Older people are a much greater proportion of the congregation in smaller churches, magnifying the difficulties of smaller churches since older people tend to have much less energy than younger people. At the same time, those aged between 25 and

34 are much more likely to be part of larger congregations – the larger the congregation the greater the percentage of those in this age-group

4

ETHNICITY AND OTHER CHARACTERISTICS OF CHURCHGOERS

The Census asked for much more than just the age and gender of churchgoers, and this chapter explores some of the other demographic factors, frequency and length of churchgoing, and distance lived from the church, all asked in Questions 10 to 13 on the form.

Frequency of church attendance

One of the questions asked on the "slip" was how frequently the individual churchgoer attended a Sunday service. Some churches, especially rural churches, only hold services once a fortnight or once a month, and sometimes a minister is not available and a service is held with a less-than-a-week frequency. The question differed slightly from that asked in 2002 when the additional numbers attending "quarterly" and "twice a year" and "once a year" were requested. This time the extra numbers coming "quarterly," "twice a year" were requested and then specifically the number coming at Christmas.

Adjusting the 2002 percentages to relate to the 2016 question shows that overall in 2016 80% of churchgoers attended at least once a week. In 2002 the percentage was 82%,[42] so the regularity of people's churchgoing habits has not changed significantly in the last 14 years. These are self-reported figures, not the minister's estimates, and may be over-inflated as a consequence.

Some attend more than once a week. That percentage was 13% in 1984, 14% in 1994,[43] 17% in 2002 and is 14% in 2016, showing the same broad figure when allowable statistical variations are taken into account. Likewise the percentage attending fortnightly was 10% in 2002 and is 9% in 2016. The proportion attending just monthly was 8% in 2002 and is 7% in 2016.[44] The 2016 percentages are shown in the pie chart, the "less frequently" indicating the proportion of occasional churchgoers who happened to be in church on Census Sunday:

Figure 4.1: Frequency of Sunday church attendance in Scotland, 2016

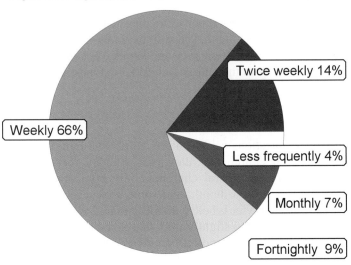

In England in 2005, the percentages were twice weekly 18%, weekly 65%, fortnightly 11% and monthly 6%. "Less frequently" was not measured.

The variation of frequency of attendance by denomination is shown in Table A3 in the Appendix and reflects the general pattern seen in 2002. Most of those attending twice weekly continue to be among the Independents (33%) and Other Presbyterians (31%), joined now by the Pentecostals (35%), followed by the Baptists (23%), as in the previous Census (when the percentages were, respectively, 26%, 35%, n/a, and 25%).

Most of those attending fortnightly were the Other Presbyterians (15%, but 7% in 2002) and Pentecostals (16%), followed by the Episcopal Scottish Church (11%, 12% in 2002) and the Church of Scotland (11%, 9% in 2002). The Roman Catholics had the smallest percentage (4%, 5% in 2002).

The monthly attenders were mostly those in the Smaller Denominations (13%, 6% in 2002), followed by the Episcopal Church (9%, 7% in 2002) and the Pentecostals (9% also). Smallest percentages (both 4%) were the Baptists and Other Presbyterians.

Many churches used the "slips" to help obtain the required information from their congregation. The letter accompanying the Census form had indicated that if collating these was too onerous the slips could always be sent back and they would be counted by the administrators. Over 2,600 slips were thus returned, some 2% of the recorded churchgoers. The advantage of this process was that an additional analysis could then be completed as it was possible to look at frequency by age of churchgoer. The results are shown in Figure 4.2:

Figure 4.2: Frequency of churchgoers by age

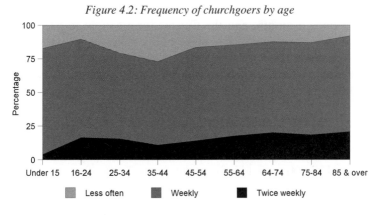

Figure 4.2 shows that those aged 35 to 44 attended church less frequently than those in other age-groups, something also found in the 2005 English Church Census. It is this age-group which is frequently looking after growing children, not all of whom may be keen on going to church. One seven year-old boy said to his father, "God is not boring, Daddy, but church is." It was the men more than the women in this age-group who particularly

attended less, perhaps because taking "time-out" with their children.

The worshipping community will be larger than those attending on any particular Sunday, and the percentages in Figure 4.1 suggest it could be up to 20% higher, that is of the order of 490,000 people.

Visitors

The average percentage of visitors in Scottish churches on 8th May 2016 was 4%, the same percentage as in 2002. The Roman Catholics and Other Presbyterians were marginally below this at 3% each, while the Episcopal Church had the highest percentage at 6%. In England in 2005 the percentage of visitors was 5%.[45]

Additional attenders

More people attend church than can be measured on a typical Sunday count such as a Census. Some come less frequently than even once a month, and the Census form sought to ascertain what these extra numbers might be by asking approximately how many extra people attended quarterly, twice a year, or at Christmas. The 2002 Census had used "once a year" instead of "Christmas". The numbers are quite significant:

- 51,000   attend every quarter, some 0.9% of the population
- 75,000   attend twice a year, 1.4% of the population, and
- 157,000   attend only at Christmas, 2.9% of the population.

There will almost certainly be some overlap in these figures and they are guestimates, not accurate counts, but they represent a substantial number of extra people who reckon on attending church at some time. If they were all different individuals they would total 5.2% of the population. That is the maximum number; if the minimum number is simply the extra coming at Christmas, that adds to a total of 10.1% of the Scottish population who attend church on at least one occasion every year. The weekly number is just over two-thirds, 71%, of this overall total.

What proportion of these additional numbers attend the different denominations? Table 4.3 shows these:

Table 4.3: Proportions of those attending church occasionally by denomination

Frequency	Church of Scotland %	Other Presbyt-erians %	Episcopal %	Baptist %	Indep-endent %	Pente-costal %	Smaller Denom-inations %	Roman Catholic %	Base (=100%)
Quarterly	41	6	6	3	10	6	9	19	51,000
Twice a year	40	1	7	1	4	4	4	39	75,220
Christmas	43	1	7	2	3	4	5	35	156,580
Average	41	3	7	2	6	5	6	30	~

The average figure shows that of the extra people occasionally coming to a church service on a Sunday, two-fifths, 41%, go to a Church of Scotland church, almost a third, 30%, go to a Roman Catholic church and the remainder to another denomination in the proportions shown. It should be noted that at Christmas, it is the National Church which attracts the largest number of occasional people; the same is true of the Church of England in England which usually attracts about 40% of those specially going to church at Christmas.

Ethnic background of churchgoers

One of the questions on the "slip" asked about ethnicity. The overall results of Question 11 are in Table 4.4 which compares the ethnic background of Scottish churchgoers with the proportions in the general population, using similar terminology, as given in the 2011 Population Census:

Table 4.4: Ethnicity of Scottish churchgoers and the Scottish population

EthnicGroup	White %	Mixed %	Black %	C/K/J %	I/P/B %	Other Asian %	Other Non-White %	Base (=100%)
Churchgoers	93.8	1.2	2.6	0.5	1.1	0.6	0.2	389,510
Population	96.0	0.4	0.7	0.6	1.6	0.4	0.3	5.3 million

Black = Black Caribbean/African/Other C/K/J = Chinese/Korean/Japanese
I/P/B = Indian/Pakistani/Bangladeshi

The population percentages are very different from those in England where many more of the immigrants have settled, where 85% are White, 8% are Asian, 4% Black, 2% Mixed and 1% Other. The figures show that in Scotland the churches have more Non-Whites pro rata than in the general population. There are more people of Mixed background in the churches (three times the population percentage), many more Blacks (almost four times the population percentage), but fewer Indians, Pakistanis and Bangladeshis (almost certainly because fewer of these come from a Christian background). The percentage of Asians overall (including the "Other Asians") and Other Non-Whites is about the same as in the population. Some of the Whites in Scotland are Polish, an unknown percentage of churchgoers, but 1.7% of the population when measured in 2014.[46]

Figure 4.5: Ethnicity proportions of churchgoers and population, Scotland, 2016

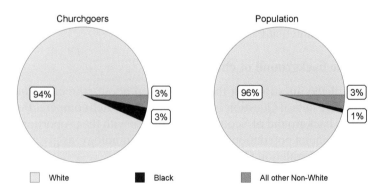

If the proportions of Mixed which are part-Black in Scotland are the same as in England, then half of the Mixed will have a Black component and, while the Church Census did not break the Mixed down, a similar proportion may be assumed. This would mean that 3.2% of Scottish churchgoers are Black, against 0.9% in the population as a whole. They are the largest group of Non-White churchgoers, as they are in England.[47] The different proportions are illustrated in Figure 4.5.

Breakdown by age

A breakdown by age for churchgoers for the different ethnicities is not robust enough as the numbers are so small, but taking all the Non-Whites together we can compare them with the White churchgoers, as in Figure 4.6:

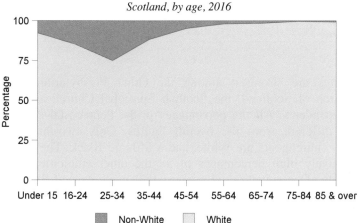

Figure 4.6: Proportions of White and all Non-White churchgoers in Scotland, by age, 2016

It is very obvious from Figure 4.6 that the Non-White churchgoers are predominantly younger than the White churchgoers – the average age of Non-Whites is 33 and for Whites it is 55! Exactly a quarter, 25%, of all those going to church in Scotland aged between 25 and 34 are Non-White as are 15% of those aged 16 to 24 and 12% of those aged 35 to 44, with smaller percentages in other age-groups.

Breakdown by denomination

The ethnicity of congregations in the various denominations is shown in Table 4.7:

Table 4.7: Scottish churchgoers by ethnicity by denomination

Ethnicity	Church of Scotland %	Other Presbyterians %	Episcopal %	Baptist %	Independent %	Pentecostal %	Smaller Denominations %	Roman Catholic %	Overall %
White	98.1	98.3	96.2	92.7	95.0	68.1	87.5	88.4	**93.8**
Black	0.6	0.4	1.8	3.3	2.7	20.9	8.4	2.8	**2.6**
Mixed	0.7	0.2	0.5	0.8	0.4	3.8	2.1	2.5	**1.2**
I/P/B	0.2	0.1	0.6	0.6	0.7	4.0	0.7	3.4	**1.1**
Other Asian	0.1	0.4	0.2	1.1	0.3	1.0	0.7	2.0	**0.6**
C/K/J	0.2	0.4	0.7	1.1	0.7	1.3	0.6	0.6	**0.5**
Other Non-White	0.1	0.2	0.0	0.4	0.2	0.9	0.0	0.3	**0.2**
Base (=100%)	136,910	17,900	13,380	17,810	30,740	18,860	18,310	135,600	389,510

Black = Black Caribbean/African/Other   I/P/B = Indian/Pakistani/Bangladeshi
C/K/J = Chinese/Korean/Japanese

Whites are strongest among the Other Presbyterians, the Church of Scotland, the Scottish Episcopal Church and the Independents. All the percentages in the Pentecostal column are different from the overall figures. Only two-thirds of their churchgoers are White, and a fifth are Black. They have relatively high percentages of all the other ethnicities. The Smaller Denominations also have a high percentage of Blacks – one person in every twelve. More than half, 54%, of all the Black churchgoers attend either a Pentecostal church or one among the Smaller Denominations. The Roman Catholic Church has many Indians, Mixed and Asian churchgoers.

What can be learned from this analysis? Why are the Pentecostals more attractive to Black people? Black immigrants tend to come from a Pentecostal background. The culture in many Black homes is an *expectation* of church attendance on a Sunday. In London, 19% of the Black population attend church against just 8% of the White. Many Black people are *enthusiastic* about evangelism, not always true of White people. Black preachers often preach long sermons, but also ones in which the implications of the passage being studied are clearly drawn out. Black people frequently have a *world* consciousness, not just a country consciousness, and teach accordingly. Black people like to attend successful churches, and growing churches are deemed successful. But perhaps the key reason, as given by a speaker for the Black churches, is that, "Evangelism is more important to them than material advancement." Their growth is not accidental, but sacrificial.

Length of time attending current church

Question 12 asked, "Please estimate roughly how many of your congregation have been coming to your church for ..." with five time periods being given. The overall answers are given in Table 4.8 .

Table 4.8: Length of time Scottish churchgoers had been attending their current church in 2016

Under 3 years %	3 to 5 years %	6 to 10 years %	11 to 20 years %	Over 20 years %	Average length	Base (=100%)
14	10	14	17	45	16 years	389,510

Almost half of those going to church in Scotland have been attending their present church for more than 20 years. Since the average age of all churchgoers is 53 (Table 3.8) this means that many started attending their present church before they were 33.

Length of time by age

The length of time a person has been attending their current church naturally varies by their age, with younger people attending for much shorter times and older people, in general, longer. Figure 4.9 shows the variations:

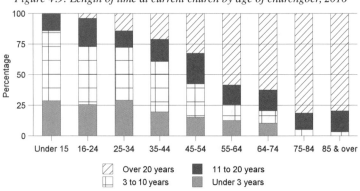

Figure 4.9: Length of time at current church by age of churchgoer, 2016

Naturally younger people have been at church for fewer years than many older people. About a quarter of those under 35 have been at their present church for under 3 years, suggesting they may have started going or that they had moved from another church, and since many will have left home while under 35 changing church is quite likely. Some have not moved – 15% of those aged 25 to 34 said they had been at their present church for over 20 years (the shaded section at the top of the 25-34 column).

At the other end of the scale nobody 75 or over had been at their church for less than 6 years, perhaps indicating a lack of outreach among older people. But there were recent arrivals, whether by conversion or house move is not known, for all ages up to 65 (the light grey section at the bottom of Figure 4.9).

It is possible to look at length of time at present church by age of churchgoer, using the percentages in Tables 3.1 and 4.8, to get the Table below.

Table 4.10: Length of time at church by current age of churchgoer

Age / Length at Church	Under 15 %	16 to 34 %	35 to 54 %	55 to 74 %	75 and over %	**Total %**
Under 3 years %	4	3	3	4	0	**14**
3 to 5 years %	4	3	2	1	0	**10**
6 to 10 years %	4	2	4	3	1	**14**
11 to 20 years %	2	2	4	6	3	**17**
Over 20 years %	0	1	5	22	17	**45**
Total %	**14**	**11**	**18**	**36**	**21**	**100**

How much successful evangelism is taking place in Scotland? If "successful" is measured by the number newly at church, under 3 years in Table 4.10, then 3 or 4% have joined a church in the last three years at all ages up to 75, though this will include those moving house, and will probably include some coming back to church after a time away.

Table 4.10 shows that 4% have been going to their church for less than 3 years for those aged under 15. Presumably if churchgoing parents move house and church, church attending children under 15 will inevitably be in that church for a short time.

Many of those present for less than 3 years will be new people, since coming back and moving house will apply to only a very few. 4% of 389,510 people at church is just over 5,000 young people a year starting church, a small rate of growth maybe but they join the 50,000 other young people already in church all under 15. Scottish church attendance may be declining but the decline is a net figure, made up of gains to the church less losses, and Table 4.10 indicates that there are some real gains from the work of mission in which most churches are engaged in one way or another.

Length of time by denomination

The figures in Table 4.8 may also be broken down by denomination, as shown in Table 4.11:

Table 4.11: Length of time in present church by denomination

Length of time in present church	Church of Scotland %	Other Presbyterians %	Episcopal %	Baptist %	Indep- endent %	Pente- costal %	Smaller Denom- inations %	Roman Catholic %	**Overall %**
Under 3 years	11	21	14	20	19	23	23	13	**14**
3 to 5 years	8	10	9	15	19	20	19	10	**10**
6 to 10 years	11	11	17	15	15	23	18	15	**14**
11 to 20 years	16	19	23	19	14	16	14	18	**17**
Over 20 years	54	39	37	31	33	18	26	44	**45**
Base (=100%)	136,910	17,900	13,380	17,810	30,740	18,860	18,310	135,600	**389,510**
Average length	18	15	15	13	13	10	12	16	**16 years**

This Table shows that the two largest churches, the Church of Scotland and the Roman Catholic Church, have the smallest percentage (average 12%) of those attending their churches who have been coming for less than 3 years, while the Pentecostals and the Smaller Denominations have the highest percentage (23% each, almost double). The latter is not just because both are strong in mission but also because they are seeing many new churches being started (they both have the highest number in Table 2.11). If these two largest groups were excluded from the figures, the overall percentages for the other denominations would be, respectively, 19%, 12%, 16%, 17% and 36%.

The Pentecostals and Smaller Denominations Churches have the smallest percentage of attenders who have been in their present church for over 20 years, on average half the percentage of those in the Church of Scotland and Roman Catholic Church. This relates to some extent to the age structure of those attending – the Pentecostals have the highest percentage of those aged 35 to 64 (Table 3.8), an age range in which many people move house for family or employment reasons. It may also be that with fewer older people in their congregations, decisions on change or mission may perhaps be made and accomplished more easily.

The differences in this Table are really quite substantial with respect to church dynamics and church culture. One large Scottish church which had a separate survey in 2013 found a similar result to the Church of Scotland in terms of percentages of length of attendance, although it wasn't a Presbyterian church. On seeing the results the minister said, "Now I know why decisions to change things are so difficult; from now on I am going to focus on evangelism." He had a large number who had been in the church a long time, and he needed more younger people in his congregations who could be trained to be replacement leaders.

Distance lived from the church

The final question in the section on "People" on the Census form asked the respondent to indicate roughly how far those in their congregation lived from the church, three distances being taken – under half a mile (which may be taken perhaps as walking distance), between half a mile and 3 miles (which may be taken as roughly the immediate sphere of influence, or parish) and over 3 miles. The distances necessarily are approximate, but they give a helpful indication of how far people have to come, and the necessity for transport if the distance is a long one. The overall results were:

- 27%   lived under half a mile away
- 50%   lived between half a mile and 3 miles away, and
- 23%   lived more than three miles away.

The question was not asked in previous Scottish Censuses, so no earlier comparisons can be given. It was asked in the London Church Census when the results were, respectively, 32%, 44% and 24%,[48] results of the same order of magnitude.

Distance by age

The variation by age of attender was relatively small as Figure 4.12 indicates:

Figure 4.12: Distance churchgoers lived from their church by age, 2016

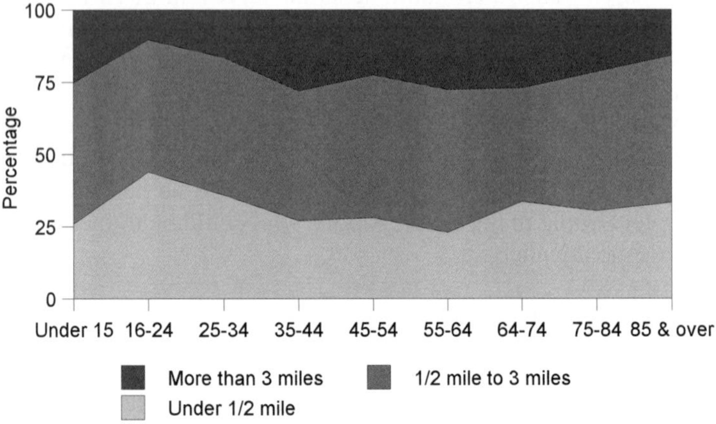

Those aged 16 to 24 tended to live closest to the church they attended, presumably because they could walk or cycle, and likewise those 85 or over were less likely to live more than 3 miles away, though some did.

Distance by denomination

Table 4.13 shows the variation of the percentages given above by denomination. The Table reflects the Parish system of the Church of Scotland and Roman Catholic Church as both these have the highest percentage of attenders living under half a mile from the church; it also reflects the high percentage of elderly people attending the Church of Scotland churches (Table 3.8).

Table 4.13: Distance churchgoers lived from their church by denomination

Distance lived from church	Church of Scotland %	Other Presbyterians %	Episcopal %	Baptist %	Indep-endent %	Pente-costal %	Smaller Denom-inations %	Roman Catholic %	**Overall %**
Under ½ mile	31	22	17	15	22	19	22	28	**27**
½ to 3 miles	51	52	49	52	42	39	44	52	**50**
Over 3 miles	18	26	34	33	36	42	34	20	**23**
Base (=100%)	136,910	17,900	13,380	17,810	30,740	18,860	18,310	135,600	**389,510**

The Baptists, Scottish Episcopal Church and the Pentecostals have the lowest percentage of those living reasonably close to their church, the strength of attending a particular church of their denomination making people willing to travel some distance to get to it. The London Census showed that those attending particular churches (especially if they were ones using their language) were willing to travel sometimes quite long distances in order to get there. The same will probably be true in Scotland where churches of overseas nationals are located, although whether services were translated into different languages from English was not asked as it was in the London study.

So what does all this say?

In this chapter we have looked especially at the ethnicity of Scottish churchgoers, and also other characteristics. Two-thirds of Scottish churchgoers go every week, something which has not changed since the last Census and seems to be generally true of churchgoers in the UK. The other third go at different frequencies, half attending more frequently, the other half less often.

On Census Sunday, 8th May 2016, taken as an average Sunday, the percentage of visitors attending Scottish churches was 4%, the same as in 2002. Occasional churchgoers come perhaps once a quarter or twice a year, but Christmas visitors are quite high, some 3% of the total population, meaning that 10% of Scottish people are in church at this time. This is obviously a key opportunity for churches in their communities.

Almost 19 out of every 20 people attending church in Scotland in 2016 were White. Of the remaining 6%, two-fifths were Black, a proportion coming to church much higher than their relative numbers in the general population, and representing more than a quarter, 27%, of all people of Black ethnicity in Scotland. Just 7% of White people attend, and 8% of all other ethnicities. Non-White people aged 25 to 34 make up a quarter of all those of that age in church. A fifth, 21%, of Pentecostal church attenders are Black, and 8% of those in the Smaller Denominations. Pentecostals and Roman Catholics have a relatively high percentage of Indian people and those of Mixed derivation attending their churches. The Church of Scotland and Other Presbyterian churches both have the highest percentage of White people attending, 98%.

On average people had been attending their current church for 16 years, an average which varied by denomination, with Pentecostals and Smaller Denominations both having a much smaller average because so many new churches in these two groups have been started in the last few years. The Church of Scotland and the Roman Catholic Church had the highest percentage who had been present for more than 20 years (on average, 49% of their attenders). Somewhat naturally, the older a person the more likely they were to have been in their present church for longer.

On the other hand, an analysis of length of attendance by age of attender showed that new people were joining the church every year, especially about 5,000 young people under the age of 15. This is good news!

Half the churchgoers in Scotland lived between half a mile and three miles away from the church they attended, with the remaining half split almost equally between those living nearer and those further away. Older people and those aged 16 to 24 were most likely to live nearer. Those attending Baptist, Episcopal, Church of Scotland or Pentecostal churches were least likely to live close by.

5

CHURCHMANSHIP OF SCOTTISH CHURCHGOERS

Churchmanship is a church's "ethos" and was first asked in the 1994 Census. Ministers or others completing the form were asked to tick up to three boxes describing their congregation's theological position (not their own, which may be different): Anglo-Catholic, Broad, Catholic, Charismatic, Evangelical, Liberal, Low Church, Radical, Pentecostal, or Other (please specify). Many Scottish respondents wrote in words like Traditional, Reformed, Presbyterian, Church of Scotland, and so on in the last box. A complete list of the ticks given by combination are given in *UK Church Statistics* No 3.[49] Four churches ticked four boxes not three; what they wrote in "Other" was therefore ignored.

These words were not defined in any way on the form or on the Scottish Churches' special website. They would therefore almost certainly have slightly different meanings for ministers of different theological persuasions. This means that the tables giving their numbers or percentages will not be a collection of totally homogeneous answers but those which to a greater or lesser extent are partially heterogeneous.

These ticks were then turned into one of six "churchmanship" groups which are used for analysis purposes. These groups, determined by the various tick combinations made, are: Broad, Liberal, Reformed, Evangelical, Low Church or Catholic. "Catholic" is not synonymous with "Roman Catholic" although the majority of Roman Catholic churches did so describe themselves. A number of Scottish Episcopal Churches described themselves as Catholic, as did a few Church of Scotland and those in the Smaller Denominations. Some Catholic churches described themselves as Liberal or Broad and a few (four) as

Evangelical. Those indicating they were "Pentecostal" were always treated as Charismatic.

As there are many Evangelical congregations these were broken down further into three groupings: Reformed Evangelical, Mainstream Evangelical and Charismatic Evangelical. "Reformed", "Evangelical" and "Charismatic" were either boxes for ticking or for writing in under "Other", and those ticking or writing these were classified as such. "Mainstream" is not one of these words, but is used to differentiate those ticking just "Evangelical" from the other two groups to save confusion. Those called "Mainstream Evangelicals" have nothing necessarily to do with Anglican and Baptist organizations using the word "Mainstream" in their name although there may be some connection in practice. Some in the Mainstream category prefer to call themselves "Conservative."

Churchmanship of Churches

Table 5.1 gives the number of churches in each churchmanship in Scotland, and shows that in 2016 two-fifths, 40%, of the churches in Scotland described themselves as Evangelical, followed by a sixth, 17%, who were Reformed, and 13% who were either Broad or Catholic. These percentages had not changed greatly since 2002 or 1994, though the proportion of Mainstream Evangelical churches was growing because of the increase in the number of Pentecostal churches in that period, virtually all of which were Evangelical. Pentecostals have now been separated from them, as described in Chapter 2.

Table 5.1: Churchmanship of Scottish churches, 1994 to 2025E

Churchmanship	Evan: Reformed	Evan: Main.	Evan: Charis	Evan TOTAL	Reformed	Low Church	Liberal	Broad	Catholic*	Total
1994	618	670	281	1,569	668	239	486	576	626	4,164
2002	594	694	276	1,564	667	239	484	573	617	4,144
% change 02-16	-23	+8	+1	-5	-7	-12	-15	-19	-19	-11
2016	**460**	**747**	**278**	**1,485**	**620**	**210**	**411**	**465**	**498**	**3,689**
2025	401	773	281	1,455	603	200	384	426	452	3,520
1994 % of total	15	16	7	38	16	6	11	14	15	100
2002 % of total	14	17	7	38	16	6	12	13	15	100
2016 % of total	**12**	**20**	**8**	**40**	**17**	**6**	**11**	**13**	**13**	**100**
2025 % of total	11	22	8	41	17	6	11	12	13	100

*Not to be identified solely with the Roman Catholic Church

Churchmanship by Denomination

A breakdown of the churches by denominations shows that:

- The number of Evangelical churches in the Church of Scotland has increased slightly to one-fifth, 20%, of the total
- Three-quarters, 77%, of the Evangelical churches which are Other Presbyterian are Reformed Evangelical
- Three-quarters, 77%, of the Baptist churches are Mainstream Evangelical
- Nine-tenths, 90%, of the Independent churches are Evangelical, and of these a quarter, 24%, are Charismatic Evangelical
- Half, 53%, of the Smaller Denominations churches are Evangelical
- Five-sixths, 86%, of Roman Catholic churches are Catholic as are a fifth, 22%, of Episcopal Church of Scotland churches

The only churchmanship to see a significant increase in its proportion of churches since 2002 was the Mainstream Evangelical (up from 17% in 2002 to become 20% of all the churches), with more of these churches than before in the Church of Scotland (50% increase [from 67 congrergatons to 101 in 2016] to be 7% of all their churches), Other Presbyterian churches (22% increase to be 18% of the total), Episcopal Church of Scotland (up 50% to be 8% of their total), Baptist churches (up 7% to be 77% of all Baptist churches) and the Roman Catholics, with 4 such churches out of 476, up from 3 in 2002.

Free Church of Scotland

Part of the growth in the Other Presbyterian group of churches is especially seen in the Free Church of Scotland. The Rev Fergus MacDonald, a former Moderator, comments, "Free Church growth can be partly accounted for by the emergence of a stronger missional outlook over the past decade which has prompted congregations to serve the community where they are located, and has also created a sense that decline is not inevitable. Having said that, Free Church growth is concentrated in about 15% of congregations that are witnessing significantly increased attendance and membership. ... The ethos of the denomination today is more mission-oriented than at any time in my 50+ years in the Free Church ministry."[50]

Some of the Free Church of Scotland churches hold services in the afternoon as well as morning and evening. When services were held was not a question asked in this Census, but their figures show that it is their morning congregations which are growing, as shown in Figure 5.2:

Figure 5.2: Attendance at Free Church of Scotland Sunday Services,
2008 to 2015E

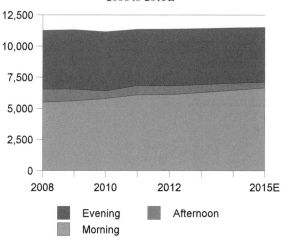

Churchmanship of Churchgoers

The question on a church's ethos was not asked on the "slips", so the answers are those given by the minister or person completing the form, not individuals in the congregation. It is assumed in the following analysis that all those in a particular church are of the churchmanship persuasion given by the minister, something almost certainly not true. However, when surveys have been taken of churchmanship by asking individual attenders, it has usually been found that between two-thirds and three-quarters of a congregation are of a similar churchmanship description to that given by the minister. There is therefore a certain amount of "swings and roundabouts" in the attendance numbers in each category of churchmanship. Table 5.3 below gives the overall churchmanship of Scottish churchgoers.

Table 5.3: Churchmanship of Scottish churchgoers, 1994-2025E

Churchmanship	Evan: Reformed	Evan: Main.	Evan: Charis	Evan TOTAL	Reformed	Low Church	Liberal	Broad	Catholic*	Total
1994	79,930	67,840	31,190	178,960	107,570	29,790	69,300	84,100	221,490	691,120
2002	62,060	72,580	28,560	163,200	85,050	23,880	51,710	62,390	183,900	570,130
% change 02-16	-44	+4	+2	-15	-42	-40	-47	-44	-32	-32
2016	**34,540**	**75,520**	**29,030**	**139,090**	**49,100**	**14,390**	**27,380**	**35,080**	**124,470**	**389,510**
2025	19,260	74,740	30,490	124,490	32,580	11,070	14,150	19,150	91,060	294,500
1994 % of total	12	10	4	26	16	4	10	12	32	100
2002 % of total	11	13	5	29	15	4	9	11	32	100
2016 % of total	**9**	**19**	**7**	**35**	**13**	**4**	**7**	**9**	**32**	**100**
2025 % of total	7	25	10	42	11	4	5	7	31	100

* Not to be identified solely with those attending Mass at Roman Catholic churches

Table 5.3 shows that in total the Evangelicals have only declined at half the rate across all churches between 2002 and 2016 (-15% compared with -32% in the "% change" line). Within the Evangelical group, it is the Reformed Evangelicals which have dropped most, paralleling the decline in the Reformed group (-44% and -42%). Churches whose ethos is Low Church, Liberal or Broad have also declined at much the same percentage as Reformed. The Catholics, who are 97% Roman Catholics, 2% Episcopal and 1% others, have declined at a slower rate, the same rate as overall, -32%. Mainstream Evangelicals and Charismatic Evangelicals have grown slightly, reflecting the rise of the Pentecostals, although these are only a quarter, 25%, of all Charismatics.

Table 5.3 projects the figures forward to 2025, and it is the Evangelicals which seem likely to increase further in proportion to the whole, even though overall numbers in 2025 are projected to decline from those in 2016. In 2016, a third, 35%, of Scottish churchgoers were Evangelical, but, if the forecast becomes roughly true, that will increase to two-fifths, 42%.

The following Table puts the number as the percentage of the total number of churchgoers in each denomination.

Table 5.4: Churchmanship of Scottish churchgoers by denomination, 1994-2016

Denomination	Year	EvanRe-formed %	Evan Main stream %	Evan Charis %	Evan TOTAL %	Re-formed %	Low Church %	Liberal %	Broad %	Catholic %	**TOTAL =100%**
Church of Scotland	1994	17	4	2	23	34	8	11	23	1	293,170
	2002	17	6	2	24	34	8	11	22	1	228,500
	2016	12	15	3	30	30	7	9	21	1	136,910
Other Presbyterian	1994	68	12	0	80	18	1	0	1	0	23,310
	2002	61	17	0	78	20	1	0	1	0	22,170
	2016	58	24	0	82	16	1	0	1	0	17,900
Episcopal	1994	1	9	10	20	9	8	21	21	21	20,350
	2002	2	9	12	23	6	7	25	20	18	18,870
	2016	2	8	17	27	5	6	26	18	18	13,380
Baptist	1994	18	66	14	98	0	0	2	0	0	24,530
	2002	16	66	16	98	0	0	2	0	0	24,830
	2016	14	69	16	99	0	0	1	0	0	17,810
Independent	1994	12	48	28	88	4	1	6	1	0	48,020
	2002	10	55	24	89	3	1	5	2	0	45,010
	2016	6	61	25	92	3	1	3	1	0	30,740
Pentecostal	2016	10	45	40	95	0	0	1	4	0	18,860
Smaller[1] Denominations	1994	8	31	23	62	3	6	15	12	2	32,020
	2002	6	34	25	65	3	7	15	9	1	28,640
	2016	8	32	29	69	3	7	11	9	1	18,310
Roman Catholic	1994	0	1	0	1	0	1	10	2	86	249,720
	2002	0	2	0	2	0	1	7	2	88	202,110
	2016	0	3	0	3	0	1	6	1	89	135,600
TOTAL	1994	12	10	4	26	16	4	10	12	32	691,120
	2002	11	13	5	29	15	4	9	11	32	570,130
	2016	9	19	7	35	13	4	7	9	32	389,510

[1]Included Pentecostals in 1994 and 2002   Evan = Evangelical

This shows the trends more clearly, and several are noticeable:

1. The proportion of Scottish churchgoers who are Evangelical has been increasing over the last 20 years, whereas the other types of churchmanship are either static or declining. Catholic churchmanship, a very important and large segment of the whole, similar to the proportion of Evangelicals, has not changed proportionately but remained at a third of the total, 32%, nor has the Low Church percentage changed (a much smaller 4%).

2. Reformed, Liberal and Broad have all declined in percentage of churchgoers, from two-fifths, 38%, in 1994 to just under a third, 29%, in 2016. This may be related both to the age spectrum and size of these congregations.

While Table 5.4 gives the trends it is difficult to see the broad proportions just for 2016 which are given in Table 5.5 below, without the breakdown for Evangelicals. The shaded squares are where the percentages are significantly larger (in two cases smaller) from the overall proportions given on the bottom line.

Table 5.5: Proportions attending church on Sunday by denomination and churchmanship, 2016

Denomination	Evangelical %	Reformed %	Low Church %	Liberal %	Broad %	Catholic %	Base (=100%)
Church of Scotland	30	32	7	9	21	1	136,910
Other Presbyterian	82	16	1	0	1	0	17,900
Episcopal	27	5	6	26	18	18	13,380
Baptist	99	0	0	1	0	0	24,830
Independent	92	3	1	3	1	0	30,740
Pentecostal	95	0	0	1	4	0	18,860
Smaller denominations	69	3	7	11	9	1	18,310
Roman Catholic	3	0	1	6	1	89	135,600
All Scotland	**35**	**13**	**4**	**7**	**9**	**32**	**389,510**

Evangelical Roman Catholics

The very large majority of Roman Catholics described themselves as having Catholic churchmanship (89% in Table 5.4), something to be expected and which has been true of every Census. However, a very small number of Roman Catholics describe themselves as Evangelical, a number which is slowly growing, up a quarter, 28%, to 3,600 in 2016 from 2,800 in 1994.

The Census form did not ask them whether they were part of a group with charismatic gifts or would otherwise be among those referred to in the June 2016 letter from the Congregation for the Doctrine of the Faith in Rome entitled *Iuvenescit Ecclesia* ("The Church Rejuvenates"), a document seeking to include such groups as "more mainstream in the life of the Church," according to Brendan Leahy, Bishop of Limerick.[51]

They are nearly 3% of all the Roman Catholics in Scotland and nearly 3% of all Evangelicals, percentages very similar to those in England in 2005.[52] There is, however, no significant difference between their age structure and that of congregations generally, though they do attract more families (proportions of those aged 35-44 and children are higher from Table A8 in the Appendix). The Evangelical Roman Catholic churches are much larger than the average Roman Catholic Church though not the largest. All these churches had run an Alpha Course at some stage.

Churchmanship by Gender of Churchgoer

Table 5.6 gives the breakdown of churchmanship by gender, an analysis not given in either 1994 or 2002.

Table 5.6: Churchmanship by Gender of Scottish Churchgoer, 2016

Churchmanship	Evan: Reformed	Evan: Main	Evan: Charis	Evan: TOTAL	Reformed	Low Church	Liberal	Broad	Catholic	Total
Male	13,730	31,190	13,150	58,070	17,670	4,950	6,190	12,910	54,900	154,690
Female	20,810	44,330	15,880	81,020	31,430	9,440	21,190	22,170	69,570	234,820
Overall	**34,540**	**75,520**	**29,030**	**139,090**	**49,100**	**14,390**	**27,380**	**35,080**	**124,470**	**389,510**
Male % of total	*9*	*20*	*9*	*38*	*11*	*3*	*4*	*8*	*36*	*100*
Female % of total	*9*	*19*	*6*	*34*	*13*	*4*	*9*	*10*	*30*	*100*

This Table shows that there are slightly more Evangelical men than Evangelical women (38% to 34%, with most of the difference being more Charismatic men), rather more Catholic men than Catholic women (36% to 30%), and twice as many Liberal women as Liberal men (9% to 4%). The other churchmanships did not vary greatly by gender.

Churchmanship by Age of Churchgoer

Similar information is also available by the age of churchgoers, and this is given in Table 5.7:

Table 5.7: Churchmanship by Age of Scottish Churchgoer, 2016

Age of churchgoer	Evan: Reformed %	Evan: Main. %	Evan: Charis %	Evangelical TOTAL %	Reformed %	Low Church %	Liberal %	Broad %	Catholic %	Overall %
Under 5	4	4	6	5	3	2	3	3	4	4
5 to 11	7	9	10	9	6	6	5	6	8	8
12 to 15	3	4	5	4	2	2	2	2	3	3
16 to 24	4	5	10	5	2	2	2	2	6	4
25 to 34	5	6	12	7	3	2	3	4	9	6
35 to 44	7	7	12	8	5	4	4	5	11	8
45 to 54	9	11	14	11	8	7	7	8	12	10
55 to 64	15	14	13	14	15	15	13	15	15	14
65 to 74	22	21	11	19	26	29	29	27	18	22
75 to 84	19	14	6	14	23	24	24	21	11	16
85 and over	5	5	1	4	7	7	8	7	3	5
Base (=100%)	34,540	75,520	29,030	139,090	49,100	14,390	27,380	35,080	124,470	389,510
Average age	55	51	40	50	60	62	62	60	49	53

This Table helps explain some of the previous findings. The Charismatic Evangelicals, two-thirds of whom are Pentecostal, have by far the youngest profile with an average age of just 40 (Pentecostals' average age was 39, Table 3.8). Younger people have more energy, so the fact that they have a third of their congregations aged between 16 and 44 (34% against 18% average) helps to explain their growth.

At the other end of the scale, those in Low Church and Liberal congregations are by far the oldest (60% or 61% 65 and over against 43% average), with an average age of 62, which will almost certainly mean problems with continuity and retaining congregations in the next 10 or 20 years. Those in Reformed or Broad congregations are similar, with an average age of 60 (and 56% or 55% 65 or over) which will mean similar problems in due season.

The two largest groups, the Evangelicals as a whole and the Catholics, are remarkably similar in age composition, though the Evangelicals have more children (18% under 16 to 15% Catholics), while the Catholics have 20% aged between 25 and 44 to the Evangelicals 15%. The Evangelicals also have more aged 75 to 84 than the Catholics (14% overall to 11%), made up mostly from the Reformed and Mainstream Evangelicals. The Reformed Evangelicals are not as elderly as their Reformed counterparts but are similar, an average age of 55 to 60, but only 46% 65 or over compared to 56%.

Churchmanship by Congregational Change

Table 2.9 showed how congregational change had varied since 2011 by denomination; the next Table does it by churchmanship:

Table 5.8: Change in congregational size over last five years

Churchmanship	Evan: Reform'd %	Evan: Main. %	Evan: Charis %	Evan TOTAL %	Ref- ormed %	Low Church %	Liberal %	Broad %	Catholic %	**Overall %**
Increased significantly	24	20	34	24	4	5	12	7	8	**14**
Increased slightly	15	13	24	16	9	15	15	13	14	**14**
Remained fairly static	20	25	22	23	27	24	28	32	29	**26**
Decreased somewhat	34	35	19	31	51	49	39	43	39	**39**
Decreased significantly	7	7	1	6	9	7	6	5	10	**7**
Base (=100%)	460	747	278	1,485	620	210	411	465	498	**3,689**

It may be seen from Table 5.8 that it is the Evangelicals who said their congregational size had increased significantly since 2011 (24% in total against an average of 7% for all the other groups). It is especially the Charismatic Evangelicals which have seen significant recent increases in their congregations. This increase is especially led by the Pentecostals, 44% of whose churches are Charismatic, and by the Independent churches, 24% of which are Charismatic Evangelical.

The percentage of static churches was similar whatever the churchmanship. Fewer Evangelical churches had decreased, but three-fifths of Reformed (60%) and Low Church (56%) congregations had seen a decrease since 2011. About half of Broad (48%) and Catholic (49%) congregations had decreased also.

So what does all this say?

The churchmanship of churches and churchgoers is quite different from each other largely because the Catholic churches (89% of which are Roman Catholic) are so much larger than most other Scottish congregations. So while only 15% of churches are Catholic, some 32% of churchgoers are Catholic. At the other end, 40% of churches are Evangelical but just 35% of churchgoers.

Nevertheless, the Catholic proportions of either churches or churchgoers have not changed significantly in the last 22 years, whereas the Evangelical proportion of churchgoers has grown from 25% in 1994 to 35% in 2016. Likewise, the total of Reformed, Liberal and Broad churchgoers has dropped from 38% to 29% in this period while their combined total of churches has remained the same at 41%.

The Evangelical growth may be seen among both the Mainstream Evangelicals and the Charismatic Evangelicals, both of which have almost doubled in percentage terms between 1994 and 2016 (from 10% to 19% and from 4% to 7% respectively). This growth is not seen just in percentage terms but in actual numbers, moving from 96,760 people in 1994 to 101,270 in 2016, a real growth of +5%.

Reformed Evangelicals, like the Reformed, Liberal and Broad churchgoers have declined, both in percentage terms and actual numbers – from 50% to 38%, or 345,560 people to 148,010, a decline of -57%.

Although their percentages have remained the same, Catholic

and Low Church together have gone from 248,800 people in 1994 to 140,220 in 2016, a decline of -44%.

These changes are reflected somewhat in the average ages of the three groups: Mainstream and Charismatic Evangelicals are 48 years on average, while Reformed Evangelical, Reformed, Liberal and Broad average 59 years while Catholic and Low Church average 50 years. Growth therefore on one level seems to be strongly age related.

Growth is not gender related. There are more Charismatic and Catholic males than females, but twice as many female Liberals than male. It is, however, related to churchmanship, since it is predominantly the Evangelical churches which have seen growth, as measured in significant percentage increases of congregations, especially among the Charismatic Evangelicals (Pentecostal and Independent denominations particularly).

6

THE GEOGRAPHY OF SCOTTISH ATTENDANCE

The country of Scotland is divided into small civil geographical units like every other country, which in Scotland are called Councils. The number of churches, the population of each Council for each Census year and total church attendance are given in *UK Church Statistics*. Table 6.1 on the next page shows what percentage the churchgoers are of the population in each Council for each Census year and forecast through to 2025.

Percentage attending church

No Council reached 50% response rate (the overall average was 40%) but Aberdeenshire did best with 49%, followed by Fife with 48%, and Highland and Clackmannanshire both with 46%.[53] Some respondents were kind enough to explain the detailed circumstances of the rural churches of which they had oversight. The number of small churches in areas like Highland and Argyll and Bute is remarkable and they draw small but regular groups of worshippers if not every week, then fortnightly or monthly, such as on the islands of Colonsay and Oronsay. It is thought Columba landed on Oronsay on his way to Iona from Ireland in the middle of the 6th century.[54] Such churches in other parts of Highland can form the base for Pilgrimages such as that advocated around the village of Killin, a small village at the Falls of Dochart, with a "spectacular series of rapids," at the western end of Loch Tay, encompassing 7 rural churches, taking 5 hours if cycling.[55]

Church attendance in every Council has decreased between 2002 and 2016 except one – Aberdeenshire where attendance grew by 2%. This is almost certainly because of the many Polish workers employed by the oil industry or in other areas such as military bases. As already noted in Chapter 2, there are

Table 6.1: Percentage of the population attending church in each Census year, and numbers

Council	1984 %	1994 %	2002 %	2016 %	2025E %	2002 numbers	% change 2002-16	2016 numbers	2016 churches
Aberdeen City	9.9	8.9	7.7	5.7	5.1	16,180	-19	13,050	117
Aberdeenshire	15.2	12.0	9.5	8.4	7.6	21,690	+2	22,040	228
Angus	9.9	8.9	6.8	4.7	3.6	7,390	-26	5,490	107
Argyll & Bute	10.5	8.9	7.4¹	5.3	3.9	6,790¹	-32	4,650	77
Clackmannanshire	16.4	12.5	10.1	5.3	2.9	4,830¹	-46	2,590	34
Dumfries & Galloway	14.2	11.3	8.6	4.5	2.6	12,800	-47	6,820	133
Dundee City	14.6	12.2	9.7	6.4	4.7	14,030	-33	9,470	90
East Ayrshire	16.4	13.0	11.2	6.6	4.5	13,610¹	-40	8,120	80
East Dunbartonshire	21.9	16.9	13.2	7.5	4.4	14,260	-44	8,020	51
East Lothian	12.5	9.6	7.6	4.5	3.1	7,070¹	-35	4,630	57
East Renfrewshire	18.3	16.2	13.4	8.0	5.8	12,210¹	-39	7,460	31
Edinburgh City	12.5	11.6	9.0	6.5	5.4	40,670	-20	32,420	219
Eilean Siar (Western Isles)	68.3	58.7¹	55.5¹	44.3	38.7	16,120	-25	12,020	141
Falkirk	15.6	12.7	9.7	5.5	3.4	14,100	-40	8,420	78
Fife	11.8	9.7	8.0	4.5	3.3	28,040	-38	17,440	223
Glasgow City	22.2	16.3	14.1	10.3	6.8	82,750	-26	60,890	361
Highland	21.0	16.6	14.0	9.6	7.6	29,410¹	-23	22,530	362
Inverclyde	22.6	20.0	17.1	10.4	6.7	14,340	-42	8,250	51
Midlothian	13.8	10.6	8.4	4.8	3.2	6,600¹	-36	4,210	52
Moray	17.8	13.4	10.5	6.7	5.1	9,170	-30	6,450	97
North Ayrshire	15.9	12.5	10.8	6.6	4.5	14,670¹	-39	8,980	92
North Lanarkshire	24.0	18.5	16.2	8.9	5.8	52,360	-42	30,250	182
Orkney Islands	15.4	14.9	12.9	9.7	8.6	2,480	-15	2,100	39
Perth & Kinross	12.8	11.8	10.0	6.9	5.7	13,520	-23	10,390	140
Renfrewshire	22.8	20.2	16.7	10.7	7.7	28,650¹	-35	18,690	97
Scottish Borders	13.6	11.6	9.0	6.0	4.7	9,730	-29	6,910	111
Shetland Islands	16.2	13.9	13.2	9.1	7.4	2,890	-27	2,110	45
South Ayrshire	18.5	14.6	12.6	7.4	4.9	14,110¹	-41	8,300	59
South Lanarkshire	13.3	12.2	9.5	5.6	3.7	28,870	-39	17,610	139
Stirling	17.6	13.4	10.8	5.4	3.1	9,350¹	-46	5,050	64
West Dunbartonshire	21.1	13.2	11.2	6.2	2.9	10,470	-47	5,580	52
West Lothian	12.5	9.4	6.8	4.8	3.5	10,970	-22	8,570	80
Overall	**16.9**	**13.6**	**11.2**	**7.2**	**5.3**	**570,130**	**-32**	**389,510**	**3,689**

¹ Revised figure

27 Polish churches in Scotland, and many Poles are Roman Catholic.

Eilean Siar Comhairle nan (or the Western Isles, but now usually abbreviated to Eilean Siar) continues to have the highest church attendance rate in Scotland, although it has reduced from two-thirds, 68%, in 1984 (when it also included Skye and the District of Lochalsh) to 44%, in 2016, and is projected to fall a little further. It remains, however, the stronghold of the Free Church of Scotland (whose attendance is three-fifths, 61%, of the total). After Eilean Siar, the next best Councils for church attendance were Inverclyde, Glasgow City and Renfrewshire, all with 10% or more of their population, all three being strongly Roman Catholic Councils. The Roman Catholic Bishop of Paisley, John Keenan (Paisley is the largest town in Scotland with 75,000 people) was very unhappy with a 2016 survey which described the Ferguslie Park area of the town as the "most deprived in Scotland" because it suffered disproportionately from poverty and crime.[56]

Those with the smallest church attendance were Angus, Dumfries and Galloway, East Lothian, Fife, Midlothian and West Lothian, all six with just under 5% of their population going to church on a Sunday. Three Councils are projected to have less than 3% attendance by 2025 – Clackmannanshire, Dumfries and Galloway (the lowest at 2.6%) and West Dunbartonshire. In 2025, the Orkney Islands are expected to have the highest percentage going to church after Eilean Siar, some 9% of its tiny population then of 22,000. Although of similar size in terms of population, the Shetland Islands have a smaller percentage going to church in 2016 and this is projected to fall faster than in the Orkneys.

As in rural counties in England, rural Highland has a relatively small population (4% of the total Scottish population) but it attracts nearly 10% of all those going to church. Rural communities are often extremely loyal to their church.

The percentages in Table 6.1 are illustrated in Figures 6.2 and

6.3 for 2002 and 2016.

Figure 6.2: Percentage attending church in 2002

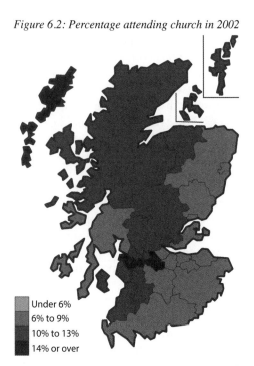

Under 6%
6% to 9%
10% to 13%
14% or over

The Table shows the strength of church attendance in the northwest and southwest of Scotland and on the Islands in 1984, which changed to being mostly the northwest by 1994 and 2002 apart from the Roman Catholic strip of Inverclyde, Renfrewshire and Glasgow City. By 2016 much of the southern half of Scotland was seeing less than 10% in church on a Sunday outside the Catholic strip, with a similar picture in 2025.

Clackmannanshire and Stirling have both seen their percentage of the population attending church drop by half between 2002 and 2016. If current trends continue, Dumfries and Galloway will have the smallest percentage of attendance in 2025, something perhaps echoed by the December 2016 edition of *Dumfries and Galloway Life*, which in its Christmas issue makes no mention of church services or celebrations anywhere in its 180 pages.[57]

Figure 6.3: Percentage attending church in 2016

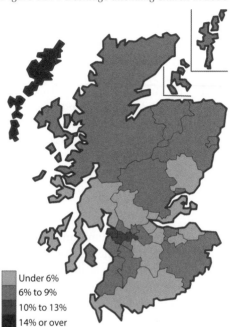

Under 6%
6% to 9%
10% to 13%
14% or over

Dunfermline was the old capital of Scotland. Rev Allan Vint undertook a local Census in the years 2009 to 2011 just for the Church of Scotland Dunfermline Presbytery. He found that in 2011 those attending these Church of Scotland churches on a Sunday were 1.9% of the population, one third of the 6.0% proportion in 1984. Estimating the total attendance in Fife for 2011 from Table 6.1 would give 5.7%, showing that the Church of Scotland in that year accounted for a third of all the Sunday worshippers.[58]

Variation by Churchmanship

The combined Evangelical percentage, at 40%, is the highest of any churchmanship category overall, but it varies considerably. It is highest in Midlothian and Eileen Siar where in both

Councils 54% of churches are Evangelical, followed by 53% in Falkirk and 51% in Inverclyde, the only four Councils over the half-way mark. On the other hand just 20% are Evangelical in Perth and Kinross, 21% in Scottish Borders and 28% in Clackmannanshire, the lowest three. Evangelicals are strongest in the north of Scotland, and the cities of Aberdeen, Dundee and Edinburgh.

Churches which are Broad or Liberal made up a quarter, 24%, of Scottish churches in 2016, and are especially strong in Clackmannanshire, East Lothian, and the Orkney Islands. They are fewest in Midlothian, North Lanarkshire and West Dunbartonshire. Their strength is seen in the south east of Scotland and they are weakest in the Roman Catholic "corridor" running from Inverclyde and Renfrewshire east towards Edinburgh.

A sixth, 17%, of Scottish churches are Reformed which excludes a further 12% defined as Reformed Evangelicals and included under the latter. They are strongest in the central Councils of Scotland and are 30% of all churches in East Renfrewshire, 27% in Perth & Kinross and 26% in both Angus and East Ayrshire, the Councils with the highest percentage. The lowest is in Glasgow City with just 6%.

One church in eight, 13%, in Scotland describes itself as "Catholic," a term not to be confused with Roman Catholicism especially since other churches use the same term to describe themselves. Catholics are strongest in the Roman Catholic corridor between Glasgow and Edinburgh and also Aberdeenshire (23%) because of the Poles.

Evangelicals are concentrated more in the cities of Aberdeen, Edinburgh and the North-West, Catholics around Glasgow and the North-West, those who are Broad/Liberal more in the centre and South-East of Scotland, and those who are Reform broadly North and South-West.

Churchgoers who are Liberal or Broad are strongest in the

Islands and central Scotland outside the Glasgow-Edinburgh belt of Councils, where they are generally fairly weak as a percentage of the population. Reformed churchgoers, on the other hand, are strong in the north of Scotland (except Moray) and also in East Ayrshire, the Renfrewshires and the Scottish Borders.

Variations by Age of Churchgoers

The age of those attending church in Scotland varies quite considerably according to where a church is located. Broadly speaking, urban churches, such as those in Aberdeen, Dundee, Edinburgh and Glasgow have the largest proportions of younger people (under 16),[59] and this is also true of Aberdeenshire and the Orkney and Shetland Islands. The average age of churchgoers is lowest in the four cities and Aberdeenshire. Only a third, 34%, of churchgoers in these five Councils are 65 and over, against an overall average in Scotland of two-fifths, 43%.

The Church Army launched the Dundee Centre of Mission in September 2014 in Scotland's fourth largest city, especially to help meet some of the problems of homelessness experienced there.[60] There is also a youthful belt stretching from Glasgow to Edinburgh as well as in the Orkney Islands and Western Isles.

The oldest churchgoers are in the rural areas of Angus, Clackmannanshire, Dumfries and Galloway and North Ayrshire, all four Councils having an average age of 60 or more. Dumfries and Galloway has the oldest average age, 64, where three-fifths, 61%, of its churchgoers are 65 or over.

The overall pattern that is being shown here is that younger people who go to church are much more likely to do so in urban areas where they presumably live because of employment, Aberdeenshire being the exception as a Council attracting many younger people because of its nearby oil industry and perhaps because of some of the military bases. The percentages are quite striking – over the whole of Scotland some 18% of churchgoers are aged 16 to 44. In Aberdeen City, Aberdeenshire and Edinburgh that percentage is 27% for each, 25% for Dundee and 24% for Glasgow, all percentages significantly above the average.

The contrast is with the rural Councils of Dumfries and Galloway where just 7% of their churchgoers are between 16 and 44, Clackmannanshire with 8% and North Ayrshire with 9% (the lowest three), and others not far behind – 10% in Angus and the Shetlands, 11% in Perth and Kinross and the Scottish Borders, and 12% in the Orkneys and Inverclyde.

This urban/rural divide is seen in England too, although accentuated by the extreme position of London which attracts almost a quarter, 24%, of that nation's entire churchgoing population![61] Other major cities like Birmingham and Manchester also tend to have more thriving churches, while rural areas such as Cornwall or Norfolk have many elderly people attending church.

Rural churches tend to have small congregations, often share a minister with other groups, may have services only fortnightly or monthly, but those attending them frequently have a strong tenacity to "hang on" and the small isolated country churches are still regularly used by the faithful. As transport to these churches becomes more difficult for them, people perforce are unable to attend as often as they did or would like to, but they do not stop believing simply because they do not now go to church. They become part of what Steve Aisthorpe has called "The Invisible Church" which, while his research was initially focused on the Highlands and Islands area, it is also true for many other areas as subsequent research showed.[62] He found very large numbers of people (44% of the population) who would form part of such a church.

Are there ways, perhaps electronic ways, by which they may still be incorporated into groups for fellowship and friendship? In some places people are already experimenting with Worship-via-the-web, such as *Sanctus Media*, led by a former Moderator of the General Assembly, the Very Rev Albert Bogle. Should they be counted in a Church Census? Maybe, but they weren't on this occasion.

Variations by Length of Attendance

It is the cities which not only have more younger people but, by direct analogy, also the highest proportions of those who have been in their present churches for the shortest time. The same Councils have the fewest percentages of churchgoers who have been present for 20 years or more, but in addition to Aberdeen, Aberdeenshire, Dundee, Edinburgh and Midlothian, there is also Stirling (but not Glasgow).

There are six Councils where more than half of all their churchgoers have been attending their current church for over 20 years, most but not all, in the south west of Scotland: North and East Ayrshire, Inverclyde, Renfrewshire, Clackmannanshire and the Shetland Islands. All of these except the Shetland Islands are especially strong in Roman Catholic numbers, and Roman Catholics appear to move less frequently than those of other denominations. Could they therefore be part of the reason why those in these Councils have been attending the same church for such a long time?

There is roughly a north-south divide in Scotland over length of attendance at the same church; those in the northern half are less likely to have been going for many years, while those in the southern half have.

The longest average length is in the Shetlands where the average is 20 years, and the shortest (13 years) in both Aberdeen and Aberdeenshire.

Variations by Denomination

The variations of denominational church attendance are kept last in this chapter as most of these will probably be already familiar to readers. In the 2002 Census the Island of Skye and the District of Localsh were included with the Western Isles but their numbers have now been removed and placed with Argyll and Bute and Highland respectively. The latter two Councils were given together previously and have now been separated.

The Councils with the largest proportions of the relevant population attending church for each are:

- Church of Scotland — Eilean Siar (7.9%), Orkney Islands (6.4%) and Aberdeenshire (4.6%)
- Other Presbyterians — Eilean Siar (27.3%), Highland (1.9%) and Argyll and Bute (1.1%)
- Scottish Episcopal Church — Edinburgh City (0.7%), Highland and Scottish Borders (both 0.6%)
- Baptist Churches — Orkney Islands (1.0%), Shetland Islands (0.9%), Edinburgh City and Inverclyde (both 0.6%)
- Independent Churches — Shetland Islands (1.2%), South Ayrshire (1.1%), and Aberdeen City, East Ayrshire and North Ayrshire (all 1.0%)
- Pentecostal Churches — Aberdeen City (1.3%), Inverclyde and Renfrewshire (both 0.8%)
- Smaller Denominations — Shetland Islands (2.7%, which includes several Methodist Churches), Inverclyde (1.0%) and Falkirk (0.7%)
- Roman Catholic Church — Eilean Siar (7.9%), Glasgow City (6.4%) and North Lanarkshire (4.8%).

So what does all this say?

This chapter has looked at church attendance geographically across Scotland. Eilean Siar dominates as it has by far the highest proportion attending, and is the citadel of the Free

Church of Scotland. No other Council comes anywhere near its 44% of the population in church on a Sunday. The Roman Catholics are especially strong in Glasgow and its surrounding Councils like Inverclyde and Renfrewshire. Churchmanship strengths follow the denominational pattern.

The Orkney and Shetland Islands also have good attendance, helped by being relatively small, compact communities with a strong churchgoing tradition. The National Church, the Church of Scotland, unlike any other denomination, has a solid presence in every Council, with the lowest percentage of the population in any Council attending on a Sunday being Falkirk with 1.4% (the lowest Roman Catholic percentage being the Shetland Islands with 0.5%).

These basic strengths (and weaknesses) play across some of the other variables measured in the Census, such as age of attender and their length of attendance at their present church.

This all simply illustrates what is already known in that geographical location is a key variable in ascertaining attendance, or the cessation of attendance by "invisible" Christians (as Steve Aisthorpe has illustrated).

Tables giving the percentages or numbers behind the various statements made about Councils are too long for easy inclusion in a small book. They have therefore been placed in *UK Church Statistics* No 3 2018 Edition,[63] together with coloured maps illustrating some of them.

7

LEADERSHIP IN SCOTTISH CHURCHES

The Census form asked a number of questions about leadership – the number of churches for which an individual minister was responsible, their age and gender, year of appointment, whether the church had a youth worker (and if so, whether full-time or part-time). These are the questions considered in this chapter. It will be appreciated that not every denomination has ordained clergy so the generic word "leader" is used throughout here. On the form the phrase "(senior) leader" was used as some churches have more than one minister.

Number of Leaders

A quarter, 25%, of the Census returns did not answer the question about the leader of their church. Whether this was because they had none at the time (being supervised by an Interim Moderator or other individual), or were sharing a leader with another church, or did not recognize any individual as the overall leader is not known. The total number of leaders was not requested, so the number in an individual church was not assessed.

The highest percentages not answering the question came from the Roman Catholics (34%) and the Independent Churches (32%). The Scottish Episcopal Church, Smaller Denominations and the Other Presbyterians were all 22%, Baptists were 17%, the Church of Scotland was 15% and Pentecostals 10%. Overall this would suggest a general shortage of church leaders as it is unlikely that as many as 25% of the total would be in transition from one congregation to another.[64]

Gender of Church Leader

One-fifth of church leaders were female, 21%, and therefore four-fifths, 79%, were male. This varied by denomination and churchmanship as shown in Table 7.1:

Table 7.1: Gender of church leader by denomination and churchmanship

Denomination	% Male	Churchmanship	% Male
Church of Scotland	70	Reformed Evangelical	86
Other Presbyterians	88	Mainstream Evangelical	87
Episcopal	71	Charismatic Evangelical	81
Baptist	100	Total Evangelical	86
Independent	85	Reformed	75
Pentecostal	85	Low Church	79
Smaller Denominations	62	Liberal	65
Roman Catholic	100	Broad	66
Overall	**79**	Catholic	89

The overall percentage across the UK in 2015 was also 79% male.[65] In 2005 the English Church Census found that female ministers were more likely to serve in remoter rural areas,[66] but this would not appear to be so in Scotland. More than 85% of ministers in the Highlands are male. There is in fact a kind of east-west divide across Scotland where male ministers are more likely to serve in Western Councils and female ministers (while still a minority) more likely in Eastern Councils.

There was a tendency to appoint women ministers to smaller churches (or male ministers to larger churches). Three-quarters, 77%, of ministers of congregations of 150 or fewer were men (so 23% women) but nine-tenths, 90%, of congregations with more than 150 people had a male minister (so only 10% women). However, almost two-fifths, 37%, of congregations of over 150 are Roman Catholic whose priests are always male. If one leaves out the Roman Catholics, then it is still true for all the other denominations put together that 85% of their larger churches (150 or more) are led by a male minister.

Age of Church Leaders

The question broke down ages into groups as elsewhere when asking for age on the Census form. The numbers by denomination are shown in Table 7.2:

Table 7.2: Age-group of church leaders, by denomination, 2016

Denomination	Under 35 %	35 to 44 %	45 to 54 %	55 to 64 %	65 to 74 %	75 & over %	Base (=100%)	Average age (yrs)
Church of Scotland	2	9	27	48	12	2	1,277	57
Other Presbyterian	9	17	26	30	14	4	232	54
Episcopal	2	8	19	46	21	4	236	59
Baptist	9	11	33	29	16	2	154	54
Independent	5	14	18	21	28	14	308	60
Pentecostal	0	20	20	34	20	6	155	57
Smaller Denominations	4	12	29	46	7	2	235	55
Roman Catholic	4	21	31	13	21	10	314	56
Overall	**3**	**12**	**26**	**38**	**16**	**5**	**2,912**	**57**

The average age of Scottish church leaders was 57, and this varied very little by denomination. Baptist and Other Presbyterian leaders were slightly younger, Scottish Episcopal and Independent church leaders on average slightly older. One seventh, 15%, of all leaders were under 45, while almost a fifth, 21%, were serving beyond the normal retirement age of 65. A tenth of Roman Catholic priests, 10%, were 75 or over, as were 14%, one in seven, of Independent church leaders.

The average age of an English church leader in 2005 was 54; the average age of a Scottish churchgoer was 53 (Table 3.8). All this is much-of-a-muchness. Table A4 in the Appendix gives leaders' age by churchmanship, but the variations are not significant. Figure 7.3 compares the ages of adult churchgoers (from Table 3.8) and leaders.

With two-fifths, 38%, of leaders currently aged between 55 and 64, there are likely to be hundreds of retirements over the next ten years. It may be, however, that lay leaders in the congregations could take up some of their responsibilities. The age of senior leaders was not requested in the 2002 Census which focused instead on lay leadership.

The average age of a leader varied across the country. The youngest leaders were in Aberdeen City, East and Mid Lothian, West Dunbartonshire and East Ayrshire, with the oldest being in Aberdeenshire, Angus, Argyll and Bute, Scottish Borders and the Shetlands as well as Councils near to Glasgow.

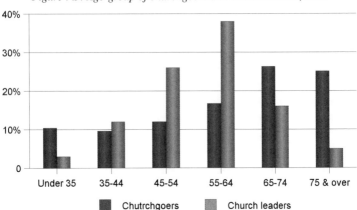

Figure 7.3: Age-group of churchgoers and church leaders, 2016

Length of time in current position

Question 5 also asked the year in which the current senior leader of a church had been appointed, which allows an estimation to be made for length of time in their current church. The average length was 8 years; in 2005 in England it was 7 years.[67]

Table 7.4: Length of time leader has been in present church by denomination

Year of appointment	2012 or later %	2007-2011 %	2002-2006 %	1997-2001 %	1992-1996 %	1991 or earlier %	Base (=100%)	Average length in years
Length of time in current posting	Under 5 years	5 to 9 years	10 to 14 years	15 to 19 years	20 to 24 years	25 years or over		
Church of Scotland	42	27	12	9	5	5	1,277	8.4
Other Presbyterian	50	23	9	10	4	4	232	7.6
Episcopal	58	19	10	8	2	3	236	6.6
Baptist	36	31	15	10	0	8	154	8.8
Independent	33	27	9	6	11	14	308	11.1
Pentecostal	37	16	19	6	3	19	155	11.2
Smaller Denominations	54	21	10	6	5	4	235	7.2
Roman Catholic	61	27	8	3	0	1	314	5.2
Overall	**46**	**25**	**11**	**8**	**4**	**6**	**2,912**	**8.1**

Almost half of all leaders, 46%, had been in their current church for under 5 years, but for some of these this will be because the church is not yet 5 years old! Table 9.5 indicates that 94 (22 + ½ of 144) churches have been started since 2012 which would reduce this percentage to 43%. A quarter, 25%, of leaders have been in position for between 5 and 9 years and the same will apply, reducing to 21% if the 109 new churches started between 2007 and 2011 were excluded.

Table 7.4 shows that 10% of leaders have been in their current church for 20 years or more. While succession of suitable leadership is always a concern, some general research on this issue shows that finding a successor able to take over a thriving church becomes more difficult if one leader has served for more than 10 to 15 years.[68]

Research undertaken for the Springboard organization in 2000 evaluating church growth from the English Church Censuses showed that the optimum time for churches to grow is when leaders have been in their church for between 7 and 9 years[69] – the average length of time as it happens that Scottish leaders have been serving from Table 7.4. It also showed that leaders staying less than 6 years or longer than 17 years were most likely to see their congregational numbers decline. Leaders serving in larger churches tend to stay longer than those serving in smaller churches.

Table 7.4 also shows that there is much variation between denominational practice in terms of service by leaders. While the average length of time served may be 8 years, it is much more than that in Independent and Pentecostal churches – perhaps because there are fewer churches in these denominations to which leaders could readily move after they have been leading one church for a long time. Many of the churches included in these two groups do not come from very large denominations, or have the difficulty of succession because the current leader may be the person who started the church originally.

On the other hand, Roman Catholic priests would seem to be

moved on after a much shorter time in a particular parish.

Table A5 in the Appendix gives similar information broken down by churchmanship, but the average length of years served does not vary significantly by church ethos. Charismatic church leaders tended to serve slightly longer than others.

It is possible to check whether the rate of change in Council numbers attending church (as shown in the map in Figure 2.3) and the length of time in which a minister has served in his/ her present church are linked – does a longer period of service mean church decline is lessened? The evidence from the 2016 Scottish Census suggests that it does not.[70] Did the length of time a minister was in post vary significantly by the number of churches looked after? Again the answer was negative. Nor did length in post vary by gender.[71]

The Councils where ministers had served the longest were those south and south-west of Glasgow, Dundee, Dumfries and Galloway and the Shetland Islands.

Drawing a horizontal line across Scotland just north of Dundee divides the country into two, the top half of which mostly shows church ministers who have been in post for under 7 years, while to the south of that line, on average they are mostly all longer, Inverclyde and Mid and West Lothian being the exceptions.

Successful long-term ministry

The following comments taken from a 2013 survey may be helpful. In order to serve for, say, 10 years, a leader must have a goal, or target, or vision at which to aim. After 10 years that vision needs renewing. Some leaders seem able to do this, and thus open up the possibility of a successful long-term ministry, while others are not able, for whatever reason, and probably need to move on to another church or challenge.

The book *God's Questions*[72] gives some suggestions as to how a "second vision," as it is called sometimes, can be developed.

This is not easy, but it may help to think through answers to questions like:

- What do you observe to be the key problems in your area of ministry (the church in general or the areas of expertise you have in your organization)?
- If you could change one thing about your present position, what would it be and why? (In other words, localise the problem as well as observing it in general terms; the answers may not be the same).
- What is the biggest hindrance you currently face with respect to evangelizing your local community? [This is a church question; if you are an agency, substitute whatever is your key task.] What could you do to remove or at least reduce its impact?
- If resources were not a hindrance, what innovative feature would you bring in over the next 6 months?

This latter question is especially important as the thinking in it begins the process of strategy and with that the opportunity for vision. The answers to the questions need to be discussed with others in the church. Part of the task is to try and envision people to think beyond the obvious – not just to go faster down the existing track, but to branch out on a new track (or tack) altogether. Sometimes we also need to look backwards in order to focus forward more clearly. "Anyone wishing to see what is to be," said Machiavelli, "must consider what has been."[73]

Number of churches for which responsible

Two-fifths, 43%, of Scottish leaders were responsible for more than one church, compared with 32% in England in 2005.[74] The overall percentage varied by denomination:

- 56% Roman Catholic
- 54% Scottish Episcopal Church
- 49% Church of Scotland
- 32% Other Presbyterians
- 29% Smaller denominations (of whom Methodists were 100%)

- 18% Pentecostal
- 14% Independent churches
-   2% Baptist churches

The percentages by churchmanship follow the broad pattern of ethos and denomination. Almost two-thirds, 64%, of Low Church leaders looked after more than one congregation, 54% of Catholics, 53% of Liberals, 46% of Broad, 45% of Reformed and 39% of Evangelical Reformed leaders. These are all about double (or more) compared with the 21% of Evangelical Charismatic and 20% of Mainstream Evangelicals who looked after more than one congregation, indicating many more in these latter two groups looked after just a single congregation.

One of the conclusions from the 2012 London Church Census was that the growth seen in London between 2005 and 2012 could partly be attributed to the fact that many London ministers looked after just one congregation. Only 7% of London's churches share a minister with other congregations.[75] This broad pattern is true in Scotland also, where ministers in urban areas were much less likely to be looking after more than one congregation. In Scottish cities only 18% of churches share a minister (not as low as London's 7%), while in other Scottish areas, 56% (over three times as may) share a minister.

The average number of congregations for which they were responsible, according to the ministers who responded, was:

- 1 church   57%
- 2 churches   21%
- 3 churches   11%
- 4 churches   7%
- 5 or more churches   4%

Half of the last group of 4% were Methodist ministers.

The overall average was 1.8 congregations per minister (the English average was 1.9), but a small number of ministers had a much greater responsibility for many (usually small) congregations. Roman Catholic priests and Episcopal and

Church of Scotland ministers were most likely to be looking after 2 or 3 churches each (30%, 33% and 35% respectively, very close to the overall 32%). It was the other denominations where leaders had larger numbers to tend. Some research in 1990 showed that many ministers struggled if asked to look after more than four churches.[76]

Youth Workers

Question 4 asked if the Church had a paid Youth Worker and if so, was that person full- or part-time. It did not ask gender or age of that individual. Only one church in nine, 11%, had a Youth Worker, and of these just two-fifths 38%, were full-time, meaning 4% of churches have a full-time worker and 7% a part-time one. These percentages are not that different from churches in London in 2012, when they were respectively 7% and 6%.[77] These percentages vary as shown in Table 7.5 .

Baptist churches are most likely to employ youth workers with nearly a quarter, 23%, employing one either full- or part-time, twice the overall average. This follows English practice also.[78] Table 7.5 shows that it is the Charismatic and Mainstream Evangelical churches which are most likely to employ a Youth Worker (a finding which overlaps very closely with Baptist churches as Table 5.4 indicates). The Episcopal Scottish Church and the Roman Catholics employ fewest Youth Workers, something again mirrored in the Broad and Catholic churchmanships.

Table 7.5: Proportions of churches employing paid youth workers by denomination and churchmanship, 2016

Denomination	% Full	% Part	Churchmanship	% Full	% Part
Church of Scotland	4	8	Reformed Evangelical	4	5
Other Presbyterians	4	3	Mainstream Evangelical	9	8
Episcopal	2	3	Charismatic Evangelical	10	10
Baptist	12	11	Total Evangelical	8	8
Independent	8	8	Reformed	2	8
Pentecostal	6	9	Low Church	1	9
Smaller Denominations	4	9	Liberal	2	7
Roman Catholic	2	4	Broad	2	4
Overall	**4**	**7**	Catholic	3	3

It is the cities and other parts of Scotland where church finances are better supported where churches can afford a paid youth worker.

So what does all this say?

Only three-quarters of the forms answered the question about their leader. Of those who did, four-fifths, 79%, of leaders were male, and a fifth, 21%, female. Two-fifths were aged between 55 and 64 and a further fifth, 21%, were 65 or over. Over the next 10 years therefore many of these leaders are likely to retire. How much attention is being given to *recruiting new leadership*?

Current leaders had been in position for an average of 8 years, but half, 46%, had been there less than 5 years and a further quarter, 25%, between 5 and 9 years, leaving 29% in their present position for 9 years or more. 6% had been in the same post for 25 years or more! *Succession is therefore an issue* in many churches. What guidelines can be given to help churches with this problem?

Two-fifths, 43%, of Scottish ministers look after more than one church, on average 1.8 congregations, but 11% have four or more. Half or more of Roman Catholic, Scottish Episcopal

Church and Church of Scotland leaders look after 2 or more congregations. Only a fifth of Charismatic and Mainstream church leaders look after two or more congregations, and roughly double the overall percentage of these churches employ a Youth Worker. As a consequence it is churches with this ethos that tend to have an *above average proportion of children* under 15 attending (Table 3.8). London's church experience suggests that growth is more likely to be associated with churches having a leader whose *sole responsibility* is that congregation.

8

MIDWEEK ATTENDANCE

Three specific questions were asked about church attendance mid-week as well as asking about services held mid-week instead of on a Sunday (see Chapter 2). These questions related to cell groups, young people's groups and church-run activities. They showed that while Sunday attendance may be decreasing across Scotland's churches, there is plenty of mid-week activity!

Mid-week Worship

Many churches have a communion service, or cell groups, house groups where the Bible is often studied, or other services, and so on. Exactly three-fifths, 60%, of churches have such, slightly greater than the 56% recorded in 2002. That is much higher than the two-fifths, 42%, of churches in England in both 1998 and 2005, and almost as many as in London, 63%, in 2012. Figure 8.1 shows how this varies by denomination.

The chart shows that a greater proportion of the Smaller Denomination churches are having more mid-week meetings now than they did in 2002 (56% to 50%), Roman Catholic churches slightly more (84% to 79%) also, while Baptist churches are having slightly fewer (90% to 83%), with other denominations about the same as before.

Figure 8.1: Churches with midweek worship, 2002 and 2016

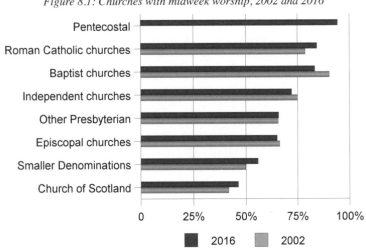

More people attending midweek

On the assumption that the churches which did not reply held midweek worship as frequently as those that did and with as many people coming on average, then overall the number of people attending midweek worship in 2016 was 75,350, or 1.4% of the population, the same fraction as in 2002, but 9% above the 69,300 attending then. Table 8.2 breaks this number down by denomination.

Table 8.2: Number attending midweek meetings in Scottish churches, 2016

Midweek meetings	Church of Scotland	Other Presbyterians	Episcopal	Baptist	Independent	Pentecostal	Smaller Denominations	Roman Catholic	**Overall**
Number attending	16,270	4,630	3,230	5,540	10,080	7,750	5,720	22,130	**75,350**
% of churches holding	46	66	65	83	72	94	56	84	**60%**
Average attendance	24	24	16	36	31	48	34	55	**34**
Aver attendance in 2002	20	24	24	33	25	n/a	24	49	**27**

The average midweek meeting in 2016 is slightly larger for

Church of Scotland, Baptist, Independent and Roman Catholic churches, much larger for Smaller Denomination churches, but smaller for the Episcopal Scottish Church. Overall these meetings are larger, up to an average of 34 people each from 27 in 2002.

Age and gender of midweek attenders

Two-fifths, 39%, of those attending midweek meetings were male, virtually the same proportion of men coming on a Sunday (40% in Table 3.1).[79] Figure 8.3 shows the age of midweek attenders compared with Sunday worshippers, where "under 25" is taken as those aged 18 to 25:

Figure 8.3: Age of midweek and Sunday attenders

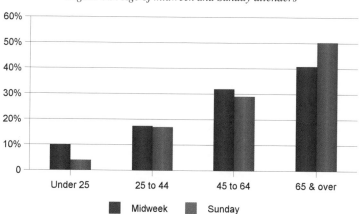

Adults attending midweek meetings are slightly younger than those going on a Sunday (56 to 68), those under 25 years of age especially favouring midweek attendance.

Percentage attending on a Sunday

The varying percentages of those attending midweek services who also attended on a Sunday are shown in Table 8.4. Overall 89% attended twice a week, meaning that midweek services attracted a further 8,290 people who came to church weekly but not on a Sunday, a further 0.15% of the population.

Table 8.4: Percentage of midweek attenders also attending on a Sunday

Midweek attenders coming on Sundays	Church of Scotland	Other Presbyterians	Episcopal	Baptist	Independent	Pentecostal	Smaller Denominations	Roman Catholic	**Overall**
% attending	87	96	81	96	93	92	91	95	**89%**

Youth Activities during the Week

Question 16a asked respondents if the young people in their church attended a regular youth activity such as Boys' Brigade, Youth Club, Brownies and so on. Half, 48%, said YES, virtually the same percentage as in 2002 (47%). This varied by denomination as shown in Figure 8.5:

Figure 8.5: Proportions of churches with young people's activities, 2002 and 2016

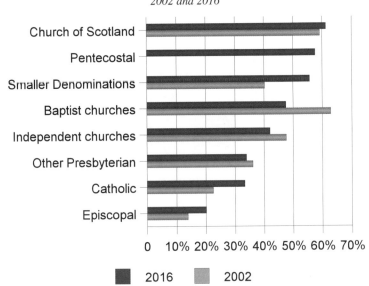

Only the Church of Scotland, Pentecostal churches and the churches in the Smaller Denominations (mostly the Salvation Army and Fresh Expressions churches in that group) had more than 50% with youth activities. It might be thought this would tally with young people in church on Sunday (as given in

Table 3.8) but while it does for the Pentecostals and Smaller Denominations, it doesn't for the Church of Scotland which has more young people coming during the week than on a Sunday. Table 3.8 does support the next two denominations, however, the Baptist and Independent churches, that is, good midweek attendance is reflected in reasonable Sunday youth attendance.

Numbers attending

This question did not ask for an age breakdown, just the total number attending under the age of 19. The average was 41 young people, a third drop from the average of 59 in 2002, but (as with the 2002 figure) this is distorted by the Church of Scotland numbers, given below. The numbers attending by denomination are shown below in Table 8.6:

Table 8.6: Numbers attending youth activities

Youth activities	Church of Scotland	Other Presbyterians	Episcopal	Baptist	Independent	Pentecostal	Smaller Denominations	Roman Catholic	**Overall**
Number attending	50,390	1,620	550	2,660	5,330	2,390	3,710	5,810	**72,460**
% of churches holding	*61*	*34*	*20*	*48*	*42*	*58*	*56*	*33*	**48%**
Average attendance	55	16	9	30	28	24	22	37	**41**
Aver attendance in 2002	70	30	31	52	37	n/a	36	35	**59**

The total number of youth attending midweek activities, 72,500 is two-thirds, 71%, of the 2002 figure of 102,000,[80] a drop of -29% which is slightly less than the decline in the overall Sunday numbers of -32% (Table 2.3). Two-thirds of this total attendance, 70%, however, is from the Church of Scotland which has always put huge emphasis on its youth activities (in 2002 this percentage was 68%). They also have a far greater number on average per church, 55, double the overall average number of 26 for all the others collectively.

Sunday attendance

Far fewer of these young people attend church on Sunday than adults coming to midweek services. Overall that percentage is 42%, leaving 58% who don't attend, or a further 42,030 young people who are involved in a church activity midweek but not on a Sunday. That is 3.7% of the population of that age-group, about half the 7.8% being reached in 2002.

This suggests less active outreach to bring in new young people in 2016 than in 2002. This is supported by the fact that in 2002 86% (100% less 14%) of those attending midweek events did not go to church, that is, they were at that stage still "outsiders", whereas by 2016 only 58% of attenders were not coming to church on a Sunday.

Why are midweek activities popular with young people? Earlier research for the Church of Scotland[81] found that:

- Youth clubs generally are "fun" (and church isn't)!
- Youth clubs usually have food available (and churches don't)!
- Young people can choose whether or not they wish to go to a youth club. While they invariably will go, *they* have the choice. When taken to church by their parents, they don't have that choice (and consequently often leave when parents eventually do give them the choice).
- Parents are not involved at youth club, so they can "be themselves", whereas in church their parents are somewhere around, so they usually feel more restrained.

Table 8.7: Percentage of young people also attending on a Sunday

Young people coming on Sundays	Church of Scotland	Other Presbyt- erians	Episcopal	Baptist	Indep- endent	Pente- costal	Smaller Denom- inations	Roman Catholic	**Overall**
% coming	30	70	48	62	47	85	55	64	**42%**

Apart from the Church of Scotland, the lowest percentages, all about 50%, are the Episcopal Church, the Independents and the Smaller Denominations churches. The largest are the Pentecostals and the Other Presbyterians, with the Roman Catholics and Baptists in between.

Attendance at Church-run Midweek Activities

The final question in this section asked respondents to estimate how many people usually attended mid-week church-run activities, like Lunch Clubs, and so on, but do not normally attend worship services at any church. They were asked to exclude any outside organisations which hired or made use of their premises.

More than in 2002

Just under half the churches responding to the Census, 46%, had midweek church-run activities, and assuming a similar proportion of churches which didn't reply had such activities with the same average numbers, then the total number of people coming to the church for these activities in 2016 was 86,710, an increase of 9% over the 2002 total of 79,700.[82] Details are given in Table 8.8.

Table 8.8: Numbers attending church-run midweek activities

Midweek church-run activities	Church of Scotland	Other Presbyterians	Episcopal	Baptist	Independent	Pentecostal	Smaller Denominations	Roman Catholic	**Overall**
Number attending	44,620	3,820	4,320	5,230	12,640	3,600	9,250	3,230	**86,710**
% of churches holding	47	32	23	53	39	36	42	13	**46%**
Average attendance	56	29	37	50	58	45	62	14	**51**

Age and gender of those attending midweek

Almost two-fifths, 37%, of those attending midweek activities were male, and 63% were female, proportions very similar to the 40:60 male/female ratio seen for Sunday attendance. Figure 8.9 shows the age of those coming to these activities compared with Sunday churchgoers.

Figure 8.9: Age of those attending midweek church-run activities and Sunday worship, 2016

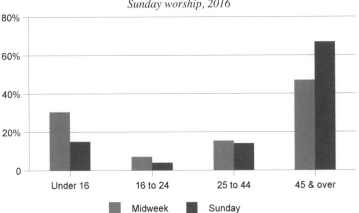

Midweek activities, which will include Fresh Expressions for a few churches, are much better at attracting children than Sunday School (or whatever it may be called) on Sunday mornings! However, midweek activities do not attract so many older people. Could midweek activities become more missional to attract those currently outside the normal ambit of church and its services?

Putting all this together

In this chapter we have looked at midweek activities by the churches in Scotland, some of which are attended by those who do not also go to church on a Sunday. The various elements looked at may be summarised in the Table on the next page.

This is an important Table as it shows that the percentage of churches having midweek services in Scotland has not changed greatly over the last 14 years though that more people attend now than before. Youth activities are held by the same proportion of churches as in 2002, but attract far fewer young people, and more of these are church young people rather than unchurched. More churches were running midweek activities in 2016 than in 2002 (a very real change in activity), but with a much lower attendance than in 2002.

Table 8.10: Summary of midweek activities by Scottish churches, 2016

Mid-week activity	% of churches having this		Average attendance		% attending on a Sunday		Total mid-week attendance Scotland 2016	Of whom attending midweek only 2016
	Scotland 2002 %	Scotland 2016 %	Scotland 2002	Scotland 2016	Scotland 2002 %	Scotland 2016 %		
Services	56	60	27	34	95[1]	89	75,350	8,300
Youth	47	48	59	41	14	42	72,460	42,000
Church-run	36	46	73	51	0	0	86,710	86,700
[1] Estimate			TOTAL midweek 2016 234,520					137,000
			Sunday attendance					389,500
			Total attendance Sunday and mid-week					526,500

The net result of this activity is that some 137,000 people enter a church space during the week who do not attend on a Sunday. That is a third, 35%, of Sunday worshippers! If one included sundry attenders then altogether over half a million people are involved with church during the normal week – almost 530,000 people. That is 9.8% of the entire population – **a tenth of Scottish people!**

The equivalent figure of the 137,000 in 2016 was 211,000 in 2002, so the 2016 percentage is a third lower, -35%, about the same as the drop of -32% in Sunday attendance. The 2002 number was a quarter, 27%, of those involved weekly with Scottish churches, and the 2016 number is a similar percentage, 26%. What this means, however, is the huge importance of midweek ministry to Scottish church life. It was so 14 years ago and has remained that way in these first years of the 21st century. It raises the obvious question of how can this fact best be exploited for the work of mission and the extension of God's Kingdom?

9

THE AGE OF SCOTTISH CHURCHES

Scotland has a rich history of churches and church life. Many would describe it as turbulent with its many controversies, splits, secessions and reunions. A diagram in Andrew Muirhead's fascinating *Story of Scotland's Churches* shows the main divergent paths which the broad Presbyterian strength has undergone in the last 300 years.[83]

Like other parts of the British Isles Scottish Christianity goes back many centuries, in fact almost two millennia. There were probably some Christians among the Roman soldiers who first occupied parts of what is now southern Scotland in the fourth century, but the main initial evangelisation came from Ireland in the fifth century. Strongly Celtic, monastic and independent from England, Christianity in Scotland birthed an uncompromising Calvinism during the Reformation in the 16th century.

The Census form simply asked the "year congregation started", but this was interpreted differently by the various respondents. While the dates given when congregations started can only relate to existing churches in current use, it therefore necessarily excludes churches which have closed. Identifying how old the existing churches are is not straightforward as some respondents gave the date their church was initially built or started several centuries ago (whatever denomination that church might now be), while others, like many in the the Salvation Army, for example, gave the date when their organisation first began its work in Scotland in the 1880s, or those in the United Free Church of Scotland who gave the date of 1929. Others gave a much later date, in the 21st century, when their congregation merged with a neighbouring congregation to form effectively a new congregation with a new beginning and not the date their church building was erected.

However, looking at a broad overview of Scottish church life according to the date of when current congregations started is perhaps helpful as it gives a sense of history on the one hand, and a perspective on new movements on the other. Table 9.1 shows the number of churches built or started by century, as given by the Census, though grossing up in this instance depends critically on the returned forms being a truly random sample of all the churches, and that may not be so.

Table 9.1: Number of churches built or congregations started by century

Year founded	C of S	Other Pres	Episcopal	Baptist	Independent	Pentecostal	Smaller Denoms.	Roman Catholic	Total	% of total
Before 1000	42	0	0	0	0	0	0	0	**42**	*1*
1000-1099	6	0	0	0	0	0	0	0	**6**	*0*
1100-1199	26	0	0	0	0	0	0	0	**26**	*1*
1200-1299	43	0	0	0	0	0	0	0	**43**	*1*
1300-1399	6	0	0	0	0	0	0	0	**6**	*0*
1400-1499	14	0	0	0	0	0	0	0	**14**	*0*
1500-1599	97	0	3	0	0	0	0	0	**100**	*3*
1600-1699	80	0	10	0	0	0	0	0	**90**	*3*
1700-1799	146	12	10	2	9	0	0	3	**182**	*5*
1800-1899	502	114	144	55	142	0	94	61	**1,112**	*30*
1900-1999	443	136	130	118	231	134	134	409	**1,735**	*47*
2000-2015	97	35	6	10	71	38	73	3	**333**	*9*
TOTAL	1,502	297	303	185	453	172	301	476	**3,689**	*100*

The figures in Table 9.1 are graphed as percentages in Figure 9.2 which also compares them with the ages of churches built in England.[84]

If these proportions are roughly correct they show the relatively large number of very old churches in England, primarily built after the invasion by William the Conqueror in 1066 when it became safe once again to live in rural areas and start villages, the relatively very few churches built in the 500 years 1300 to 1800, and the very large number of churches built and/or started in the last two centuries in both England and Scotland, though proportionately far fewer in England than in Scotland in the 20th century. In the 21st century, however, the percentage of new churches (in both countries about 9% of their current total), has been very similar, since refugees, immigrants and Fresh Expressions have come alike to both nations.

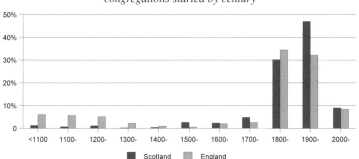

Figure 9.2: Proportions of churches built or congregations started by century

Nineteenth and twentieth centuries

Table 9.3 shows the number of churches built or congregations started in groups of 25 years (except for 2000 to 2016), with these numbers illustrated in Figure 9.4.

Table 9.3: Churches built or congregations started in the 19th and 20th centuries

Year founded	Church of Scotland	Other Pres	Episcopal	Baptist	Indep-endent	Pente-costal	Smaller Denoms.	Roman Catholic	**Total**
1800-1824	74	7	10	15	4	0	7	2	**119**
1825-1849	145	74	30	7	27	0	7	14	**304**
1850-1874	117	14	54	9	36	0	14	26	**270**
1875-1899	166	19	50	24	75	0	66	19	**419**
1900-1924	134	28	88	84	103	11	36	154	**638**
1925-1949	75	55	17	3	44	21	7	213	**435**
1950-1974	105	30	16	9	22	43	11	27	**263**
1975-1999	129	23	9	22	62	59	80	15	**399**
2000-2016	97	35	6	10	71	38	73	3	**333**
Total	**1,042**	**285**	**280**	**183**	**444**	**172**	**301**	**473**	**3,180**

The large amount of church building/planting which went on in Scotland in the first quarter of the twentieth century is clearly seen from this chart, as well as the relatively small number built in the third quarter – a complete contrast to England where a large number of churches were built to replace those bombed during WWII. The large number of Roman Catholic churches built in the first half of the 20th century is also clearly shown.

Figure 9.4: Scottish churches built or congregations started in 19th to 21st centuries

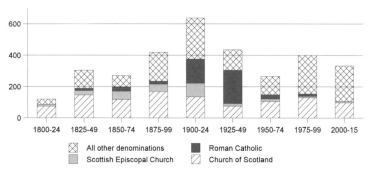

In addition, the chart reveals the very different nature of church plants being started in the 21st century where only 3% are either Scottish Episcopal Church or Roman Catholic and 29% Church of Scotland (which are mostly congregational mergers, not strictly new churches), leaving two-thirds, 68%, to all the other denominations, especially the Smaller Denominations (which includes immigrant or "Overseas National" churches), Independent churches and Pentecostals.

The 21st Century

The track of new churches started in the current century is shown in Table 9.5:

Table 9.5: Churches built or congregations started in the 21st Century

Year founded	Church of Scot	Other Pres	Episcopal	Baptist	Indep-endent	Pente-costal	Smaller Denoms.	Roman Catholic	**Total**
2000-2004	22	16	0	3	13	22	15	3	**94**
2005-2009	29	0	0	2	13	11	18	0	**73**
2010-2014	33	19	6	5	41	0	40	0	**144**
2015-2016	13	0	0	0	4	5	0	0	**22**
Total	**97**	**35**	**6**	**10**	**71**	**38**	**73**	**3**	**333**

There was a slight lull in starting new churches in the period 2005 to 2009, perhaps partly because of the recession then, but numbers picked up considerablybetween 2010 and 2014. Many of the Church of Scotland new congregations were again mergers of existing congregations. Many of the Smaller Denomination new congregations are Messy Churches which, as explained previously, exist across all denominations, with many in the Church of Scotland.

Messy Churches

A description was given in Chapter 2 of Messy Church, and because they are usually spread across several different denominations they are included together as a unit within "Smaller Denominations." They are a prominent part of a general description of church planting often now called "Fresh Expressions". Determining exactly how many Messy Churches there are in Scotland is not easy. The person who keeps a list of them at the Bible Reading Fellowship in London, Lucy Moore, reckoned there could be almost as many as 600 in Scotland in 2016, but this number is an estimate. The number included in the total number of Scottish congregations is 82 in Table 2.1, 2% of the 3,689 churches in Scotland, as these were listed on their website, a fifth of those actually in Scotland. Many churches run a Messy Church but these do not always meet monthly, and their numbers would thus be excluded from Census counts. Most churches see them as part of their normal church activities and do not reckon on them being potential church plants or new congregations. However, the official definition of a Fresh Expression is a group which has the expectation of eventually becoming a separate church congregation.

They are essentially informal gatherings where food, fun and fellowship are all important ingredients. Many families with young children are attracted to them but, in addition, many who used to attend church regularly but have lapsed (part of the "invisible" Christians already mentioned) have re-started coming to these groups. Worship and a warm welcome are key attractive characteristics.

Why should they be started? Essentially for a theological reason – God is missional and wants us prayerfully to join Him. Or, as Donald McGavran, the founder of the "church growth" movement in the 20th century, put it, "God wants His lost sheep found".[85] Fresh Expressions or Messy Church offer the gift of being community with Jesus, and are a "rounded" form of mission holding together the great commandment (to love others) and the great commission (to make disciples).[86] Also, they work – literally thousands of Messy Churches have been started in the UK in the last few years!

Denomination

Details were supplied of 123 Messy Churches and all were written to as part of the Census contacting procedure, but it was clear that about a third of these were outside the frame of reference being used. In total we received details of 32 Messy Churches, a 39% response of the 82 mentioned above. Of these, 85% were Church of Scotland (where the denomination was known), with the other 15% spread among the Baptists, Scottish Episcopal Church and the Salvation Army.

Length of time Messy Churches had been meeting

One had been started 15 years ago in 2001, and was probably originally a Church Without Walls group. Of the others, half (47%) had been started in 2012, with a quarter more recently and a quarter between 2008 and 2011. The average length of time they had been running in 2016 was 4 years, excluding the 2001 congregation; including it put the average at 5 years!

Size

The average size was 48 people. The smallest was 16 and the largest 108. A third, 32%, had fewer than 40 people, two-fifths, 39%, had between 40 and 59, and the remaining 29% had 60 or more. The Church of Scotland ones were larger than the others, 60 compared with 35. The more recently formed (since 2012) were smaller than those which had been meeting for longer, 38 compared with 60, as might be expected.

Location

Messy Church seemed to occur more in the east of Scotland than the west!

- A fifth, 19%, met in Dundee, Angus or Perth and Kinross
- Another fifth, 22%, met in Edinburgh City or Mid- or East Lothian
- A quarter, 25%, met in Aberdeen City, Aberdeenshire or Moray
- Another fifth, 19% met in Fife or Clackmannanshire
- The rest (15%) were in the Highlands, Argyll and Bute or the Orkney Islands.

Out of our very small sample there wasn't one from Glasgow, or the Ayrshires, Dunbartonshires, Lanarkshires or Renfrewshires.

Churchmanship

Not many stated their churchmanship, but by the nature of the type of activity most would see this as mission or evangelism, and would define that as Evangelical. However, there were also some, a minority, who described themselves as Liberal, Reformed or Low Church.

Leadership

Many Messy Church leaders are lay people. An analysis by George Lings of the Church Army Research Team in Sheffield found that half of Fresh Expression leaders were ordained and half were not.[87] No question was asked on lay leadership in the Census nor on leadership training, but new forms of (lay) training are emerging in Scotland.[88]

Age of attenders

As Figure 9.6 below indicates there are many more children under 12 present at Messy Church services than in services generally, which is to be expected. However, the pattern of others at these churches is very similar to the general pattern of churchgoers in Scottish churches, although they have a few more adults aged 35-44, these being the parents. It is significant that Messy Churches do not, at present, attract any greater proportion of teenagers. See Table A8 in the Appendix for details.

Figure 9.6: Age of those attending Scottish Messy Churches and all congregations, 2016

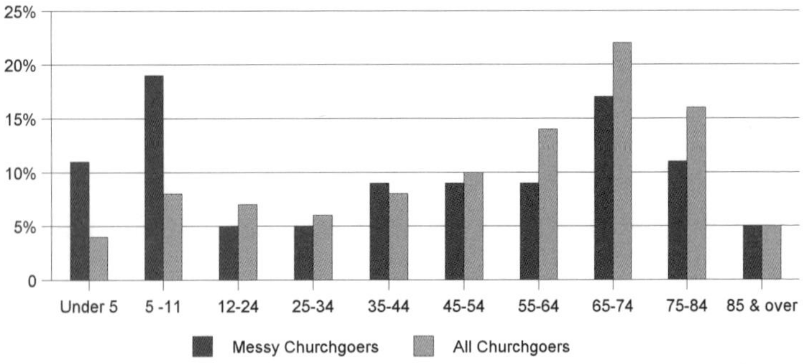

So what does this say?

Scottish churches have a very long, centuries-old, history, with 3% of the churches currently in use having been built more than 500 years ago. Three-quarters, 77%, of the current buildings, however, were built in the 19th or 20th centuries, half (47%) in the 20th century. A further 330 churches (9% of the total) have been started since year 2000. However, a third, 31%, of the Church of Scotland's congregations use a building older than 1800.

An especially large number of congregations started between

1900 and 1924, amounting to a sixth, 17%, of all churches in use today.

At least a quarter, 25%, of the congregations begun this century are Messy Churches. These focus on informality, and meeting on days or times other than on Sunday. They are popular and draw an average of 48 people each, and in total account for 1% of Scottish churchgoers. On average they are 4 years old and are likely to spread beyond the existing denominations presently encouraging them, of which the Church of Scotland is the foremost example.

10

THE LOCAL COMMUNITY
AND THE WIDER CHURCH

In order for the Scottish Church Census to be undertaken, supplementary income was needed in addition to that provided by the major denominations. Space was offered on the form for questions which would enable those participating to obtain sponsored information about their particular concerns or product without a great outlay, though they would have to wait for their private report until after the main report was completed.

We are very grateful that four organisations helped in this way – the University of Edinburgh, Alpha Scotland, Tearfund Scotland and Christian Aid. Their questions were included as Questions 18 to 24 on the back page of the Census form. The broad answers to each of these will probably be of interest to the readers of this report, so they are summarised below.

Community Engagement

"Does your church have an active programme of community engagement in any of the following areas?" was Question 18, inviting respondents to tick as many as appropriate. Six options were given, but no "Other (please specify)" for ticking. Answers are shown in Table 10.1:

Table 10.1: Community engagements by churches, 2016

Type of community engagement	Church of Scotland %	Other Presby.-erians %	Episcopal %	Baptist %	Indep-endent %	Pente-costal %	Smaller Denom-inations %	Roman Catholic %	**Overall** %
Meeting social needs	73	58	71	85	65	72	80	82	**72**
Regular neighbourhood visitation	52	54	35	20	46	34	38	62	**48**
Fair Trade	49	25	50	29	13	0	19	48	**41**
Popular or Higher Arts	15	11	32	10	6	3	12	6	**15**
Eco-Congregation Group	17	5	15	0	2	3	7	5	**12**
Street evangelism	5	11	1	15	26	55	23	9	**10**
Average	**35**	**27**	**34**	**27**	**26**	**28**	**30**	**35**	**33**

About a third of Scottish churches, 33%, engage in some kind of active community programme, the three larger denominations (Church of Scotland, Roman Catholic Church and the Scottish Episcopal Church) slightly more than others, but not significantly so.

Nearly three-quarters, 72%, of churches are involved with meeting social needs like food or housing. The Baptists undertake this most, 85%, while the Other Presbyterians do it least, 58%, still almost three-fifths involvement.

Regular neighbourhood visitation is undertaken by about half the churches overall, 48%, with Roman Catholic churches participating more than others (62%), and Baptists least (20%).

Fair Trade involvement is undertaken by two-fifths, 41%, of Scottish churches, but this varies considerably across the denominations, with no Pentecostal churches involved (0%), but almost half of the three largest denominations (all 48% to 50%).

Popular or Higher Arts was not defined on the form, and this and the remaining two types of community engagement were only undertaken by a minority of churches. Just one in seven, 15%, was involved with the Arts, which included a third (32%) of Scottish Episcopal Churches, but only 3% of Pentecostal churches and 6% of Independent and Roman Catholic churches.

One church in eight, 12%, had an Eco-Conservation group, something most popular with the Church of Scotland and Scottish Episcopal Church with 17% and 15% respectively of their churches having such a group. None of the Baptist churches had one, and only 2% of the Independent churches and 3% of the Pentecostals.

Street evangelism was the activity undertaken least by all the churches on average, just one-tenth, 10%, of them. However, this varied a great deal by denomination, with over half, 55%, of the Pentecostal churches engaged in this ministry, as well as a quarter of Independent (26%) and Smaller Denominations churches (23%).

Alpha Courses

"Has your church ever run an Alpha course (including Youth)?" was Question 19, to which the overall answer was 35% saying YES, 64% saying NO and 1% saying that they had never heard of it (an overall average but 5% of Roman Catholic churches). This compares with 38% of churches in England who said they had run an Alpha course when asked in the English Church Census of 2005.[89]

The 2016 Scottish percentage is an increase from 27% who had run an Alpha Course in 2002 (when an additional 1% also said they had run an Emmaus Course), when asked a similar question in the previous Census. This is an increase in 172 fresh churches across the 14 years between the Censuses, or an average extra 12 churches per year.

Half of the 35% of Scottish churches who had ever run an Alpha course had undertaken one in 2015, 17%. Table 10.2 shows how this is broken down by denomination:

Table 10.2: Churches which had run an Alpha course ever and in 2015

Run an Alpha course?	Church of Scotland %	Other Presby-erians %	Episcopal %	Baptist %	Indep-endent %	Pente-costal %	Smaller Denom-inations %	Roman Catholic %	**Overall** %
YES, sometime	40	15	18	65	37	58	48	14	**35**
YES, in 2015	20	8	8	36	18	23	22	5	**17**

Number of courses

The 17% of churches who said they ran an Alpha course in 2015 would equate to 630 churches running an Alpha course in Scotland in 2015.[90] However, the situation becomes more complicated as the next part of the question asked how many courses were run by each church, and how many of these were Youth courses (for those aged 11 to 18) and how many were Adult courses. Some churches would run both types, and others just one type.

Churches running Adult Alpha courses averaged 1.7 courses per church in 2015, and those running Youth courses averaged 1.1 courses per church. Some churches ran both, and we assume they averaged 1.4 courses per church. The 630 churches running an Alpha course in 2015 would then breakdown as follows:

- 100   churches just running Youth Alpha
  –> 110 such courses in total
- 250   churches running Youth + Adult Alpha
  –> 350 courses in such combinations
- 280   churches just running Adult Alpha
  –> 480 such courses in total
- Total   of 630 churches in total running Alpha
  –> Total of 940 Alpha courses run in 2015

The percentage of churches holding Alpha courses in 2015 at 17% was lower than the 27% holding them in 2002, but the 2002 question was, "Has your church ever held ...?" and did not therefore ask for a specific year, so the two percentages cannot really be compared. Nor did the 2002 Census ask about Youth Alpha.

However, the 2002 Census did ask over how many years courses had been held, the average of which was 3.0 years which, as churches had on average held 3.7 courses, suggests an average of 1.2 courses per year. If that figure is roughly correct, the 2016 results show that while fewer churches were running an Alpha course in 2016, those churches which did run at least one ran more than perhaps was the case in 2002. Alpha is being run by fewer churches but slightly more frequently, and with marginally more in attendance.

An analysis by denomination showed that Baptist churches had twice the overall average percentage of their churches undertaking an Alpha course in 2015, 36%, followed by the Pentecostals with 23%. The least were the Roman Catholics with 5%. The Church of Scotland ran the most Alpha courses per participating church, 1.6 per church, while the Other Presbyterians had least, 1.0 per church.

Attenders and Helpers

How many people came to these Alpha courses? The Youth Alpha attracted 9.3 people on average, helpers averaging 2.6 (3.5 people per helper). Adult Alphas attracted 8.5 people on average, supported by 3.1 helpers on average (2.8 people per helper).[91]

In total this meant that in 2015 some 11,000 people attended Alpha courses in Scottish churches.

In 2002 churches had been holding Alpha courses on average for 3.7 years and had seen some 46,800 people attend – an average of 12,600 per year, but that was across 27% of churches. Had only 17% of churches been holding Alpha in 2002 then the total might only have been 8,000 a year, suggesting that attendance in 2015 was much higher. Table 10.3 confirms this as it indicates courses in 2015 were attended by slightly more people on average than in 2002.

Table 10.3: Average attendance at Alpha in Scotland, 2015

Average attendance (including leaders)	Church of Scotland	Other Presbyt-erians	Episcopal	Baptist	Indep-endent	Pente-costal	Smaller Denom-inations	Roman Catholic	Overall
Youth Alpha	7	7	29	22	11	22	12	24	**12**
Adult Alpha	9	16	10	19	15	12	14	19	**12**
Average adults in 2002	13	9	12	11	14	n/a	11	10	**11**

Attendance at Youth Alpha in 2015 was in total 2,100 over 175 courses, while attendance at Adult Alpha was 8,800 in total over 765 courses.

Attendance in Table 10.3 includes those helping with Alpha. There were 500 leaders helping with Youth Alpha in 2015, meaning there were 1,600 guests, and 2,300 helping with Adult Alphas leaving 6,500 as guests. Total guests therefore were 8,100 people, or 1 person in every 670 living in Scotland, about 0.2% of the adult population.

Where Alpha courses were held

Question 19 also asked how many Alpha courses were held on the church's own premises and how many elsewhere in other venues, a question not asked in 2002.

The overall answer was that 78% of Youth Alphas were held on the church's own premises and 72% of the Adult Alphas. This varied somewhat by denomination, but perhaps the nature of the event was also important, especially for Adult Alphas, and therefore held elsewhere than the church's own premises. Not every church has a kitchen or suitable space for such occasions.

Other evangelistic courses

The final part of Question 19 asked respondents what other evangelistic courses or resources were used if they did not use

Alpha. This resulted in a wide selection of answers, by 20% of those replying, half of which were focused around one other course – *Christianity Explored*, which 10% of churches used. An overview of courses taken is shown in Table 10.4:

Table 10.4: Evangelistic courses taken by Scottish churches

Run an evangelistic course?	Church of Scotland %	Other Presby.-erians %	Episcopal %	Baptist %	Indep-endent %	Pente-costal %	Smaller Denom-inations %	Roman Catholic %	**Overall** **%**
YES, Alpha	40	15	18	65	37	58	48	14	**35**
YES, Christianity Explored	7	39	2	23	10	5	7	0	**10**
YES, other course	7	7	13	6	8	15	9	27	**10**
NO, not at all	46	39	67	6	45	22	36	59	**45**
Base (=100%)	1,502	297	303	185	453	172	301	476	**3,689**

Table 10.4 shows that the Alpha course has been run far more than any other single course, and four times more than *Christianity Explored*, although this has not been available for as long as Alpha or had such wide publicity. Other courses have also been used especially by the Roman Catholic Church, Pentecostals and the Scottish Episcopal Church. *Christianity Explored* has been largely undertaken by Other Presbyterian, Baptist and Independent churches, and not at all (or virtually so) by Roman Catholic or Scottish Episcopal churches.

Only five other courses were each mentioned by at least 10 churches – *Emmaus* (mostly the Scottish Episcopal Church), *Living the Questions* (all Church of Scotland) and *Pilgrim* (all Scottish Episcopal Church), *The God Question* (all Church of Scotland) and *RCIA* (all Roman Catholic Church).

Charity Support

Question 20 asked respondents what the characteristics of a charity were which would cause their church to be more inclined to support it, and four suggestions were made with a fifth general question. The replies were:

We are more inclined to support a charity if it ...

- 77%   Helps us direct our donations to specific projects/themes/places
- 73%   Links our faith to the issues it works on
- 40%   Helps us pray for the issues it works on
- 15%   Helps us campaign on the issues it works on
- 19%   We think financial support is more useful to charities than non-financial support.

Churches want to be able to direct their donations to a specific cause or purpose (said three-quarters, 77%) rather than just a donation to the "general fund", and they also would like their donation to link with their faith (another three-quarters, 73%). Out of the issues listed these were the key ones favoured. Baptists and Roman Catholics were especially in favour of the faith-linked issues.

Two-fifths, 40%, were seeking to link their support with their prayers, especially Baptists and Other Presbyterian churches. However, only 15% wished to see their donation linked with further campaigning or advertising, something though that the Smaller Denominations were more in favour of, and Baptists disliked. A fifth, 19%, thought financial support was more useful to charities, but since four-fifths, 81% therefore, did not tick this they presumably would support primarily non-financial giving to charities, especially Baptist churches.

Motivation to support the poor

Question 21 asked what was the church's motivation to support a charity which helps the poor. Respondents were asked to choose the three most important motives for them out of 12 possible answers. No "Other (please specify)" option was given. The results are shown in Table 10.5, although only just under half, 48%, of respondents was able to answer the question. The order (shown by the number in the first column) is the overall order found by combining all three answers.

Table 10.5: Motivations to support a charity which helps the poor

No	Motivation	Most important factor	Second most important	Third most important	Overall %
1	It helps the poor around the world	4th	1st	3rd	44
2	We give in response to a disaster	8th	2nd	2nd	38
3	We can support a specific project	5th	3rd	1st	37
4	Its vision fits with our church's vision	1st	4th	6th	35
5	Our church has traditionally supported it	2nd	5th=	7th	31
6	Our denomination supports it	3rd	5th=	10th	27
7	Someone in our church is enthusiastic about it	6th=	8th	4th	25
8	It tackles poverty holistically; body, soul, spirit	6th=	7th	8th	23
9	It helps the poor in Scotland	9th	9th	9th	16
10	A speaker gave a talk in our church about it	10th	10th	5th	15
11	I have met and trust its staff	11th	11th	11th	8
12	It provides good resources for our church	12th	12th	12th	1

The responses fell into three broad groups – those ticked by most respondents (varying from 35 to 44% of all ticks), those ticked by some respondents (varying from 23% to 31%) and those ticked by very few respondents (16% or fewer). It so happened, however, that of the factors deemed most important only one fell into the top group ("its vision fits with our church's vision").

The bottom two factors with the lowest percentage of ticks were universal across the spectrum (numbers 11 and 12). So was the ninth factor, but "a speaker gave a talk in our church about it" ranked fifth in the assessment of the third most important factor.

The top three factors were:

- Most important   Its vision fits with our church's vision
- Second factor   It helps the poor around the world
- Third factor   We can support a specific project

The motivations varied by denomination.

Involvement with Tearfund and Christian Aid

Question 22 was complicated and split between two specific charities, Tearfund and Christian Aid. The question asked 9 issues about Tearfund and 10 about Christian Aid, of which six of each were common to both of them. The overall question asked about "the level of involvement" with the two charities, and asked respondents to tick as many of the options given which were relevant to them. Table 10.6 summarises the responses given, where CAW = Christian Aid Week. The questions were found easier to answer than the previous question, and were answered by 87% of respondents.

Table 10.6: Level of involvement by church with two charities

No	Level of involvement	Tearfund %	CAW %
1	Unaware of organisation/event	5	2
2	Aware but never involved	27	17
3	Individuals support it, not the church	24	17
4	Our church has given but not in the past two years	12	7
5	Our church has given/been involved in past two years	22	54
6	An individual is a Tearfund representative/organises CAW	7	29
7	We occasionally have a speaker	12	
8	We use their prayer materials	13	
9	We use their campaign materials	10	
10	We held a CAW longer than two years ago		12
11	We have had a CAW event in the last two years		35
12	We take part in house to house collections		27
13	We have taken part in CAW in some other way		34

Both organizations are well known to Scottish church leaders, with more involved with Christian Aid Week than Tearfund. On the other hand, individuals within the church were more likely to support Tearfund than Christian Aid Week (line 3). Church's involvement with CAW was twice as much as with Tearfund (line 5), and individuals representing CAW four times more likely (line 6). Again, there is considerable variation among these answers by denomination, usually depending on their broad churchmanship.

Advocating for key issues

Question 23 asked for one of four answers to each of four questions, to which nearly two-thirds, 64%, of respondents attempted to give answers, and they sometimes gave more than one answer to a particular question. Analysis therefore is somewhat confusing! For each main question we have counted all the answers which means counting the same answer twice if given two ticks.

How were these various issues or projects supported? Table 10.7 seeks to indicate:

Table 10.7: Level of support/advocacy for various charities/projects

Cause/Project	We support this cause financially %	We advocate about this cause with local councillors %	We advocate about this cause with MSPs/MPs %	We advocate about this cause with our denomination %	Base (100%)
Local Poverty-reduction Charities	86	8	7	16	923
International Poverty-reduction Charities	84	4	5	16	926
Environmental Conservation in Scotland	15	12	17	65	319
International Environmental Projects	31	4	11	61	368

Not much advocacy takes place about local or international poverty-reduction charities, although more is undertaken within denominational boundaries. This changes with other projects, with political advocacy being highest for Scottish environmental conservation, and much denominational advocacy for this and international environmental projects.

Poverty-reduction charities do, however, attract a substantial amount of financial support from churches, with on average five in every six making donations. A third, 31%, of churches support international environmental projects, and a sixth, 15%, support Scottish environmental conservation.

These percentages varied somewhat by denomination with Smaller Denominations being much more likely to advocate the relevant cause within their denomination than others, but with the Church of Scotland being the main financial support and advocate for each of these four areas, although slightly less than others for international environmental projects.

Teaching on legacy giving

The final question on the Census form asked, "How often is the subject of legacy giving/gifts in wills spoken about in your church?" The overall answers were:

- 3%   Often
- 21%   Sometimes
- 40%   Rarely
- 36%   Never

the outcome of which indicates that this is an infrequent item on the teaching agenda! Liberal churches were twice as likely to teach this sometimes as Evangelicals (31% to 15%), but otherwise the percentages varied little by churchmanship. Figure 10.8 shows how it varied by denomination.

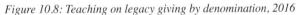

Figure 10.8: Teaching on legacy giving by denomination, 2016

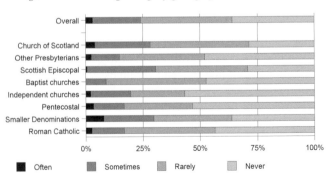

The chart shows that it is in the Church of Scotland, Scottish Episcopal Church and the Smaller Denomination churches where the subject of legacies is most likely to be raised – more than a quarter of such churches often or sometimes have such teaching. Baptist churches have this least.

The frequency of teaching is related to the age of the congregation. Table 3.8 shows that the Church of Scotland and the Scottish Episcopal Church have the highest percentage of people 65 and over (56% and 47% respectively), so the teaching is likely to be relevant to its hearers. This is not true of the Smaller Denominations, however, but "Smaller Denominations" includes the Methodist churches (one fifth of the total number) and 56% of the Methodists have such teaching often or sometimes.

Recent demographic information

The offer was made on the Census form for churches to "receive recent demographic information based on [their] postcode" and thereby giving permission for their congregation postcode and statistics to be used for research purposes. Rev Dr Fiona Tweedie from within the Church of Scotland indicated she would be willing to provide such. In the event just over half, 51%, of respondents requested such information.

So what does all this say?

This final chapter had looked at the sponsored questions which generally focused on the work of the churches in their local community. Three-quarters, 72%, of churches seek to meet local social needs and half, 48%, engage in regular visitation in their neighbourhoods. Two-fifths, 41%, are Fair Trade supporters.

A third, 35%, of churches had undertaken an Alpha course at some stage, with half of these, 17%, holding at least one Alpha course in 2015. On average both Youth Alpha and Adult Alpha courses attracted 12 people each time, marginally more than they did when a similar question was asked in 2002. The Evangelical denominations were more likely to hold such courses (three-fifths or more of the Baptist and Pentecostal churches did so). A tenth, 10%, of churches had offered *Christianity Explored* courses, especially the Other Presbyterian churches (two-fifths, 39%, having done so). Another tenth, 10%, of churches had offered some other course, especially Pentecostal and Scottish Episcopal Churches (the latter mostly being the *Emmaus* course).

Three-quarters, 77%, of churches were inclined to support a charity if it was possible to direct their funds to a specific project or theme or place, and a similar proportion, 73%, if the project could be linked to the church's faith (or standing) on the relevant issue. Churches were inclined to give gifts if such supported impoverished people internationally (rather than locally, 44% to 16%), and to respond when there was a disaster (two-fifths, 38%). Respondents put as their most important factor for giving whether the vision behind the object of their donation fitted with their church's vision.

Specific questions were asked about Tearfund and Christian Aid. Most churches had heard of one or other or both organisations, but a quarter, 27%, had never been involved with Tearfund and a sixth, 17%, with Christian Aid Week. A fifth, 22%, of churches had worked with Tearfund in the previous two years, but more than half, 54%, had been involved with Christian Aid Week in the same period. Over a quarter of churches, 29%, had someone in their congregation who helped organise Christian Aid Week, while only 7% of churches had a Tearfund representative. On the other hand, more individual congregational members supported Tearfund than Christian Aid Week (24% to 17%).

Five-sixths of churches were willing financially to support poverty-reduction charities, whether they were local (86%) or international (84%). Advocating for causes with local councillors or MSPs or MPs was undertaken by a minority of churches, though more did so for environmental conservation in Scotland than other topics. Discussion, or agitation perhaps, in their denomination was much more likely to occur, especially if the topic was Scottish or international environment projects

(65% and 61% respectively).

Teaching about legacy giving was a topic often or sometimes raised by a quarter, 24%, of churches, but was especially more likely to occur when the proportion of elderly people in the congregation was high (half or more). This teaching was primarily age-related, much more than other factors.

It may be seen that Scottish churches are active in their community work, responding positively to the topics chosen by the sponsors in relation to the questions of poverty-reduction and environmental conservation. Such actions and concerns were present whatever the denomination or size of a congregation, showing many churches have an outward focus towards their community, be that material or spiritual, the precise emphasis naturally varying with the ethos of the church.

MAKING SENSE OF ALL THIS

How can these results be used to help an individual congregation? This Appendix gives some questions to answer and then some more questions deriving from those answers. If you kept a copy of your completed Census form then get it to hand, but if not you can download a blank one from the website or send an email or letter to the contacts given at the bottom of the verso-title page.

Total number of attenders. Count how many people come to your services on a typical or average Sunday, and write the number in the box.

Age of attenders. Question 9 asked for the age breakdown of your congregation. Write these as percentages in the grid below in Line 1.

Line No	Source	<5 %	5-11 %	12-15 %	16-24 %	25-34 %	35-44 %	45-54 %	55-64 %	65-74 %	75-84 %	>84 %	Total %
1	Your church												100
2	National percentages	4	8	3	4	6	8	10	14	22	16	5	100
3	Denominational percentages												100

Line 2 gives the overall percentages for all Scottish churchgoers in 2016. Write in the numbers in Line 3 for your denomination from the relevant column in Table 3.8. Now compare either Line 2 or Line 3 with Line 1, and circle the percentage in Line 1 which is most different. If it is lower it indicates where your church is weak in comparison with others, if higher where you are stronger. How do you remedy that weakness or exploit that strength?

Write that idea down: _____

_____

Frequency of attendance. One question on the Census looked at how often people come to church (Question 10a). Express the numbers on the form from your church as a percentage of the total and put those percentages in Line 1 in the next Table. Line 2 gives the national figures. Then put in your denominational figures from Table A3 in the Appendix.

Line No	Source	Twice weekly %	Weekly %	Fortnightly %	Monthly %	Less often %	Total %	Visitors %
1	Your church						100	
2	National percentages	14	66	9	7	4	100	4
3	Denominational percentages						100	

How does your church compare? What do the differences or similarities suggest to you? Would you like to see different percentages in any box for your church? What kinds of action are appropriate to bring that change about? Write below two actions to take in the next 3 months to start that change process.

Action 1 _____

_____

Action 2 _____

_____

Size of average Sunday congregation. The next Table shows the proportions of church congregations of different sizes shown by the 2016 Census. Put a tick in the box which reflects your size in Line 1. What difference do you think size of church makes to your situation? We would all like to be larger! But is that likely in your situation? If so, write why you hope your church will grow in the next year or so and what is being done to encourage that growth. If you have a copy of your original form you may find that the answer to Question 6e is also relevant. Table A6 gives the numbers in each group by denomination. You may wish to take these numbers, expressing them as a percentage, from the appropriate column and put them in Line 3.

Line No	Source	Under 10 %	10 to 25 %	26 to 50 %	51 to 100 %	101 to 150 %	151 to 200 %	201 to 500 %	Over 500 %	Total %
1	Your church (✓)									~
2	National percentages	5	19	25	21	10	5	11	4	100
3	Denominational percentages									100

Why grow? _____

_____

How grow? _____

_____

Churchmanship. Each church has its own ethos. The next Table shows the percentage of churchgoers in each of the groups used in this Census report. Again tick the box which would correspond to your congregation. Have you seen a change over the last few years? If so, why is that, do you think? Is your church special in this regard in any way? If appropriate, write down why your church may be different from that shown for your denomination in Table 5.4.

Line No	Source	Evan Reformed %	Evan Main-stream %	Evan Charis-matic %	Evangel-ical TOTAL %	Reform-ed %	Low Church %	Liberal %	Broad %	Catholic %	Total %
1	Your church (✓)										~
2	National percentages	9	19	7	35	13	4	7	9	32	100
3	Denominational percentages										100

Why different, if at all?_____

_____

Ethnic background. One question on the Census form (Question 11) asked the breakdown of attendance by ethnic group. Express the numbers on your form as a percentage of the total and put these percentages in Line 1 in the next Table. Line 2 again gives the national figures. Look up in Table 4.7 the percentages relevant to your denomination and write these in Line 3. Some of the percentages in this Table are small, so you may need to go to one decimal place for greater accuracy.

Line No	Source	White %	Black %	Mixed %	I/P/B %	C/K/J %	Other Asian %	Other N-W %	Total %
1	Your church								100
2	National percentages	93.8	2.6	1.2	1.1	0.5	0.6	0.2	100
3	Denominational percentages								100

I/P/B = Indian/Pakistani/Bangladeshi C/K/J = Chinese/Korean/Japanese N-W = Non-White

How does your church compare? Circle the box in Line 1 where your church varies most from the national or denominational average. What do these differences imply? Would you like to see different percentages in any box for your church? What action is needed to make that change happen? Write down one action to take in the next 3 months for this purpose.

Action on ethnicity _____

_____

Mid-week worship service. Does your church have one? If so, put in the box the average attendance, and take the denominational attendance from Table 8.2.	Your church	National average	Denominational average
		34	

Mid-week youth activity. Does your church have one? If so, put in the box the average attendance, and take the denominational attendance from Table 8.6.	Your church	National average	Denominational average
		41	

Are your figures from the above two boxes more than a third different from the national or denominational figures? If so, why do you think this is? Write down your answer:

Why different? _____

_____

Summary. Of the statements you have written or boxes circled, which do you think is the most significant and why? Indicate your reason:

The most important item above for us is _____

_____

because _____

_____

Of the various actions you have indicated as worth doing in the next few months, which two have top priority? Write these down and note in your diary NOW when you will take the actions!

Priotrity 1 _____

To be completed by _____

Priotrity 2 _____

To be completed by _____

Footnote: Answering these questions and taking action on the results is more likely to be effective if done in collaboration with a colleague! This helps with objectivity and is likely to avoid procrastination!

APPENDIX: METHODOLOGY AND ADDITIONAL TABLES

In order to undertake a Census of all the churches in Scotland (or any other country) it is essential to have a complete list of all the churches, with contact details, as otherwise the study is not a comprehensive census of every single church but simply a sample of them, even if a very large sample. The list of churches compiled for the previous Censuses in 1984, 1994 and 2002 provided a headstart in obtaining a list of all the churches for the 2016 Census, but, after 14 years, many new churches had started, some churches had closed, and the minister or priest responsible for a church in almost every case had changed.

Methodology

Immediately after the meeting in February 2015 when the decision to hold a Census was taken up until the actual questionnaire was mailed to every church in March or April 2016, an intensive effort was made to ensure the list of churches on the data base was accurate, up-to-date and comprehensive. This was a long and tedious task, especially when it came to updating and/or correcting the details already held on the existing database. Many hours were spent searching the web for information.

The Church of Scotland, the Roman Catholic Church, the Baptist Union of Scotland, the Scottish Episcopal Church, the Free Church of Scotland, the United Free Church of Scotland, the Christian Brethren, the United Reformed Church and several smaller denominations were kind enough to send a complete list of their churches. Other denominations list all their churches on their website, and these were used also.

However, inevitably, with the best will in the world, some churches will have been unintentionally omitted, for which we apologise. Also as churches are starting and closing all the time, no list can ever strictly be totally up-to-date. Even the lists kindly provided by various denominations were not always entirely accurate or up-to-date.

There are at least 83 different denominations in Scotland which, as explained in Chapter 2, for convenience purposes were grouped into 8 broad sections for the Census, given in Table 2.1. The groups and the denominations making up each one, along with the number of their congregations, are given in *UK Church Statistics* No 3 2018 Edition.[92]

Grossing up for non-responding churches by denominations gives a more robust estimate than simply grossing up on the total. A like procedure was also undertaken using churchmanship as a variable, and by using the areas in which churches were based. The overall response rate was 39.8%, which rounds to 40%. This is made up from a 100% response from the London Brethren, 69% from the Seventh-Day Adventists, 67% from the United Free Church of Scotland, 61% from the Scottish Episcopal Church, 58% from the Free Church of Scotland and from the Congregational Federation, 56% from the United Reformed Church, 50% from Mountain of Fire Ministries, 45% from the Church of Scotland, 42% from Elim Pentecostal, 39% from the Baptist Union of Scotland, from the larger House Churches and of Messy Churches, 36% from the Salvation Army and smaller percentages from the other denominations.

The other two main "control" variables, as they are called, used for Census purposes were the churchmanship and locational area in which a church was situated. Most questions were analysed by these two factors. The various churchmanship combinations vary by denomination, both for churches and for churchgoers, and are given in Tables in *UK Church Statistics*.

The data on each form was entered into a computer using SPSS software which is ideal for analysis. Tables were then constructed from this software and used as appropriate. An anonymous slip was given out in many congregations for completion on Census Sunday, and the totalled numbers then inserted on the Census form.

Additional Tables

Table A1: Changes per annum in Scottish churchgoers between each Census

Age-group	Male changes per annum			Female changes per annum		
	1984-1994	1994-2002	2002-2016	1984-1994	1994-2002	2002-2016
Under 15	-3,370	-2,070	-1,360	-5,530	-1,170	-1,870
15-19	-120	-550	-480	-690	-790	-480
20-29	-490	-460	-540	-1,670	-1,870	-540
30-44	-120	-1,370	-880	-930	-3,210	-1,790
45-64	-770	-800	-1,770	-1,060	-2,940	-2,580
65 & over	+240	-190	-70	-1,750	+300	-550
Total	-4,630	-5,440	-5,100	-11,630	-9,680	-7,810

*Table A2a: Estimated number of churchgoers, by age-group, **1980 to 2030E***

Year	<10	% A	10-19	% B	20-29	% C	30-39	% D	40-49	% E	50-59	% F	60-69	% G	70-79	% H	80+	Total
1980	144,190	-37	120,900	-46	82,640	-2	90,670	-6	97,420	-1	108,500	-11	104,770	-23	86,760	-37	55,160	891,010
1990	106,200	-37	91,470	-51	64,890	-2	81,110	-14	85,170	-3	96,360	-10	96,230	-21	80,410	-30	54,890	756,730
2000	74,330	-40	66,870	-58	44,760	-4	63,830	-26	69,420	-14	82,770	-9	86,550	-15	76,210	-28	56,450	621,190
2010	48,870	-48	44,960	-59	28,260	-6	42,870	-30	47,020	-14	59,630	+3	74,970	-11	73,370	-33	54,770	474,600
2020	32,130	-62	25,350	-66	18,240	-20	26,680	-32	30,030	-14	40,060	+10	61,700	-11	66,820	-35	49,420	350,970
2030	13,450		12,060		8,520		14,560		18,050		26,250		45,830		55,410		43,650	237,780

Table A2a looks complicated, but it has been constructed by taking the numbers attending in each Census and extrapolating them by linear regression to years ending in "0" from 1980 to 2030, and then taking the age-groups thus formed into revised age-groups each of just 10 years. This means that we can see what happens to any cohort in any 10-year period.

For example, the number in the top left hand corner, "144,190" is the estimated number of children under 10 attending church in Scotland in 1980. The box to the right of that, "120,900" is the number of teenagers aged 10 to 19 attending and so on across the line. Over the following 10 years, between 1980 and 1990, all these people grew 10 years older. By 1990 the 144,190 children under 10 in 1980 had now become teenagers, but of these only 91,470 were still attending church, the number connected with a diagonal line in the column "10-19" and row labelled 1990. The number had dropped by -37%, the figure straddling the line connecting the two numbers (the figure 37 is in bold so that it can easily be seen against the slanting line). The line is inserted in that box to show the direction of change as one moves across the Table. The percentages, all in italic, show the difference between the numbers still attending after a span of 10 years. If you follow the diagonal line down from the 144,190 you come to 26,250 in the 50-59 column in the year 2030, as all those under 10 in 1980 will be in their 50s in 2030. Of the original 144,190 attending church only 26,250 will be left – a drop of five-sixths, 82%. Of course some will have died in the interim and some will have emigrated as well as some just stopping going to church. The figures are net figures as obviously some people in the right age-group will join those who have been going to church already.

Looking at the Table as a whole it may be seen that:

- Most percentages, in the columns labelled A to H, increase over the years since 1980, meaning that a greater proportion of that age-group are leaving in successive decades. This doesn't happen in columns F and G where the percentage gets less every decade. After people have been going to church for 50 years they tend not to give up the habit! The higher percentages in column H, all just under 40%, are essentially mortality rates.

• As one goes from left to right across the Table the percentages in columns B to F mostly reduce more or less successively. Those who are most lost to the church are the younger people. The Table is illustrated in part in Figure A2b:

Figure A2b: Estimated number of Scottish churchgoers, by age-group

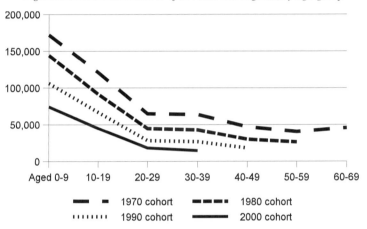

Table A3: Frequency of Church Attendance by Denomination, 2016

Frequency	Church of Scotland %	Other Presbyt-erians %	Episcopal %	Baptist %	Indep-endent %	Pente-costal %	Smaller Denom-inations %	Roman Catholic %	**Overall %**
Twice weekly	6	31	18	23	33	35	18	16	**14**
Weekly	72	48	57	63	50	35	56	72	**66**
Fortnightly	11	15	11	8	10	16	8	4	**9**
Monthly	6	4	9	4	5	9	13	4	**7**
Less often	5	2	5	2	2	5	5	4	**4**
Base (=100%)	136,910	17,900	13,380	17,810	30,740	18,860	18,310	135,600	**389,510**
Visitors %	5	3	6	4	4	5	5	3	**4**

Table A4: Age-group of church leaders, by churchmanship, 2016

Churchmanship	Under 35 %	35 to 44 %	45 to 54 %	55 to 64 %	65 to 74 %	75 & over %	Base (=100%)	Average age (yrs)
Reformed Evangelical	6	13	24	42	13	2	388	55
Mainstream Evangelical	5	12	27	30	18	8	562	57
Charismatic Evangelical	1	21	26	34	12	6	241	55
Total Evangelical	5	14	26	35	15	5	1,191	56
Reformed	2	5	29	52	9	3	471	57
Low Church	2	10	24	43	20	1	161	57
Liberal	2	12	24	40	19	3	358	52
Broad	2	9	24	44	18	3	388	58
Catholic	2	17	29	19	21	12	343	58
Overall	3	12	26	38	16	5	2,912	57

Table A5: Length of time leader has been in present church by churchmanship

Year of appointment	2012 or later %	2007-2011 %	2002-2006 %	1997-2001 %	1992-1996 %	1991 or earlier %	Base (=100%)	Average length in years
Length of time in current posting	Under 5 years	5 to 9 years	10 to 14 years	15 to 19 years	20 to 24 years	25 years or over		
Reformed Evangelical	45	24	12	9	4	6	388	8.3
Mainstream Evangelical	47	25	10	7	4	7	562	8.1
Charismatic Evangelical	41	20	12	12	5	10	241	9.8
Total Evangelical	45	23	11	9	4	8	1,191	8.7
Reformed	43	26	11	8	5	7	471	8.6
Low Church	44	27	9	4	3	13	161	9.0
Liberal	42	27	12	10	5	4	358	8.3
Broad	44	27	13	8	4	4	388	7.9
Catholic	60	25	7	4	2	2	343	5.8
Overall	46	25	11	8	4	6	2,912	8.1

Table A6: Congregations by size by denomination, 2016

Size of congregation	Church of Scotland	Other Presbyt-arians	Episc-opal	Baptist	Indep-endent	Pente-costal	Smaller Denom-inations	Roman Catholic	Over-all	Percent-age of total %
Under 10 people	25	16	46	10	35	5	47	0	**184**	*5*
10 to 25	183	83	123	25	146	26	101	14	**701**	*19*
26 to 50	399	89	84	48	101	48	87	61	**917**	*25*
51 to 100	407	60	32	49	81	41	44	61	**775**	*21*
101 to 150	196	13	4	24	42	17	12	62	**370**	*10*
151 to 200	127	16	3	3	4	13	4	18	**188**	*5*
201 to 500	164	17	7	23	39	6	1	149	**406**	*11*
Over 500	1	3	4	3	5	16	5	111	**148**	*4*
Total	**1,502**	**297**	**303**	**185**	**453**	**172**	**301**	**476**	**3,689**	**100**

Table A7: Age of congregations by size of church, 2016

Size of congregation	<5 %	5-11 %	12-15 %	16-24 %	25-34 %	35-44 %	45-54 %	55-64 %	65-74 %	75-84 %	>84 %	Base (=100%)	Average age
Under 26	*2*	*6*	*1*	*1*	*3*	*4*	*9*	*17*	*31*	*19*	*7*	20,240	61
26 to 50	*3*	*8*	*3*	*2*	*4*	*6*	*9*	*15*	*25*	*20*	*5*	39,120	57
51 to 100	*4*	*8*	*3*	*3*	*4*	*6*	*9*	*14*	*24*	*19*	*6*	92,660	56
101 to 150	*4*	*4*	*3*	*4*	*5*	*7*	*10*	*15*	*23*	*19*	*6*	66,080	56
151 to 200	*4*	*9*	*3*	*4*	*6*	*8*	*10*	*15*	*22*	*14*	*5*	42,270	52
201 to 500	*4*	*9*	*4*	*6*	*7*	*10*	*11*	*13*	*18*	*14*	*4*	78,260	49
Over 500	*4*	*9*	*4*	*8*	*13*	*14*	*13*	*13*	*13*	*7*	*2*	50,880	43
Overall	**4**	**8**	**3**	**4**	**6**	**8**	**10**	**14**	**22**	**16**	**5**	**389,510**	**53**

Table A8: Age of congregations of two particular groups, 2016

Group	<5 %	5-11 %	12-15 %	16-24 %	25-34 %	35-44 %	45-54 %	55-64 %	65-74 %	75-84 %	>84 %	Base (=100%)	Average age
Messy Church	*11*	*19*	*3*	*2*	*5*	*9*	*9*	*9*	*17*	*11*	*5*	3,900	43
Evangelical Catholics	*4*	*11*	*2*	*3*	*5*	*11*	*9*	*12*	*22*	*17*	*4*	3,560	52
Overall	**4**	**8**	**3**	**4**	**6**	**8**	**10**	**14**	**22**	**16**	**5**	**389,510**	**53**

ENDNOTES

1.   *UK Church Statistics*, No 3 2018 Edition, Edited Peter Brierley, ADBC Publishers, Tonbridge, Kent, 2017

2.   Email from a Finance Convener in a Church of Scotland congregation in the Scottish Borders, 31st May 2016

3.   Published as *Transforming Scotland, The State of Christianity, Faith and the Church in Scotland*, produced by the Barna Group in partnership with the Maclellan Foundation, 2015

4.   Wikipedia, accessed 16th September, 2016

5.   In the Presbyterian and Episcopal Churches respectively

6.   http://destiny-ministries.6net accessed 17th September 2016

7.   http://communitas.co.za accessed 17th September 2016. He has also co-authored a book with Nick Spencer, *Journeys and Stories*, published by the London Institute of Contemporary Christianity, 2006

8.   Article in *Pointers*, Journal of the Australian Christian Research Association, Vol 26, No 3, September 2016, Page 7 by Rev Dr Philip Hughes, formerly Executive Director

9.   *UK Church Statistics*, No 2, 2010-2020, ADBC Publishers, Tonbridge, Kent, 2014, Table 11.6.2

10.   Personal email, May 2016, from Rev Douglas Nicol, former Mission and Discipleship Council Convener in the Church of Scotland

11.   Details in www.communityhub.co.uk

12.   Made up from 61% from the Scottish Episcopal Church, 48% from Other Presbyterians, 45% from the Church of Scotland, 39% from the Baptists, 35% from the Smaller Denominations, 33% from the Independent churches, 23% from the Roman Catholic Church and 22% from the Pentecostal churches. See also the Appendix

13.   This compares with 9% given in the 2015 *Transforming Scotland* report (Endnote 3), based on a smaller sample

14.   *The Invisible Church*, Learning from the Experiences of Churchless Christians, by Steve Aisthorpe, Church House, Norwich, 2015, and St Andrew Press, 2016

15.   1,608 out of 4,144

16.   *Turning the Tide: The Challenge Ahead*, Report of the 2002 Scottish Church Census, Christian Research, Eltham, London, 2003, Table 4.11

17.   Based on the published figures of 4,742,800 in 1989 and 3,166,200 in 2005, as given in *Religious Trends* No 6, 2006/2007, Christian Research, Eltham, London, Table 12.2.2, although both have now been revised

18.   The 2002 figures are revised to include an additional 5,000 attenders for Other Presbyterians and 5,000 less for the Independent Churches adjusting for the estimated numbers of the Congregational Union of Scotland moving to the URC in 2000

19.   Report in the *Church of England Newspaper*, 25 April, 2014. For consistency with past Censuses, however, their numbers have been retained within the Church of Scotland total rather than included elsewhere

20.   *Prospects for Scotland* 2000, Peter Brierley and Fergus Macdonald, National Bible Society of Scotland, Edinburgh and Christian Research, London, 1995, Page 20

21. Confirmed by Rev Alan Donaldson, General Secretary of the Baptist Union of Scotland

22. *Prospects for Scotland*, Peter Brierley and Fergus Macdonald, National Bible Society of Scotland, Edinburgh and MARC Europe, London, 1985

23. So a personal email from Gregory Morris

24. Personal email from Parish secretary in Aberdeen

25. From *Religious Trends*, No 6, 2006/2007, Christian Research, Eltham, London, 2006, Table 5.15

26. Talk "Understanding and interpreting missions in the Black Christian community" on 26th September, 2006

27. Article "Identifying New Models of Church in Contemporary Australia" by Rev Dr Philip Hughes, in *Pointers*, Journal of the Christian Research Association, Vol 26, No 3, September 2016, Page 7

28. Two Census forms indicated that some in their congregation would prefer not to be designated either male or female. Since the number was very small they have been included in attendance figures but split equally between male and female. Grossed up for the whole of Scottish churchgoers this group would number less than 40 in total

29. Article "Why people stop going to church" in *FutureFirst*, June 2016, quoting surveys for Anglicans from *Statistics in Mission* for 2014 and *Christian Brethren in the UK* for 2013 for Christian Brethren

30. Three of Five Factors *Changing Women's Relationship with Churches*, www.Barna-update, 30th June 2015

31. Op cit., *Religious Trends* No 6, Endnote 17, Table 5.6.2

32. Article "The Trouble with X" by Laura Evans, *Professional Manager*, Summer, 2013, Page 58f

33. From *Hurting Elderly People & the Church*, Methodist Homes for the Aged, Christian Research, 1999

34. *Religious Trends* No 2, 2000/2001, Christian Research Eltham, London, 2006, Table 2.15, across all UK denominations, updated to 2016

35. *Some Major Religious and Non-religious Trends in the UK and Globally* 2015 to 2025 , Brierley Consultancy, Table 1.8

36. Article in *The Economist*, 27th September, 2014, Page 31

37. *The Future of Transport in an Ageing Society*, George Holley-Moore and Helen Creighton, Age UK, June 2015, Page 2

38. Church Army research can be found on their website: www.churcharmy.org.uk/ms/sc/sfc_database.aspx

39. *Winning Them Back*, Eddie Gibbs, MARC, Tunbridge Wells, Kent, 1993, Page 277

40. Op cit., Endnote 14, *The Invisible Church*, but also article in *FutureFirst*, Brierley Consultancy, October 2014, Page 1

41. U3A stands for University of the Third Age which has over a thousand branches in the UK. Most branches run special interest groups for their members, and "church-going" could almost become one of them!

42. From Table 2.12 in op cit., Endnote 16, *Turning the Tide*

43. From Page 27 in op cit., Endnote 20, *Prospects for Scotland 2000*

44. It was 6% in the *Transforming Scotland* report (see Endnote 3), Page 5

45. Op cit., *Religious Trends* No 6, Endnote 17, Table 2.7.2

46. Scottish Surveys Core Question, Scottish Government, 2014

47. Blacks were 10.4% of English churchgoers in 2005, against 6.2% of all other Non-Whites

48. *Capital Growth*, What the 2012 London Church Census Reveals, Peter Brierley, ADBC Publishers, Tonbridge, Kent, 2013, Page 110

49. To be published by ADBC Publishers, Tonbridge, Kent in 2017, Endnote 1, Table 12.21

50. Email from Fergus MacDonald, Jan 2014 quoted in op cit., Endnote 9, *UK Church Statistics* No 2, Page 10.4

51. Report in *The Tablet*, 25th June 2016, Page 12

52. Op cit., Endnote 17, *Religious Trends* No 6, Table 5.15

53. The smallest response rates were from East Renfrewshire with 20% and West Lothian with 24%

54. Scottish Natural Heritage leaflet

55. Described in detail in the *Annual Review* 2015/2016 of the National Churches Trust, July 2016, Page 28

56. Report in *The Tablet*, 17th September 2016, Page 28

57. *Dumfries & Galloway Life*, December 2016, Issue No 109 at andrea.thompson@cngroup.co.uk

58. Report *Dunfermline Presbytery Census* 2011, by Allan Vint, April 2011

59. This might possibly contribute to the fact that Dundee has the highest rate of mums-to-be abusing drugs, and the lowest employment rate in any Scottish Council in 2016 (*Report* from Dundee City Council, May 2016)

60. Article in *Share It!*, the magazine of the Church Army, Summer/Autumn 2016, Page 11

61. Op cit., Endnote 48, *Capital Growth*

62. Op cit., Endnote 14, *The Invisible Church*

63. Op cit., Endnote 49, *Church Statistics*

64. At its June 2016 Synod, the Scottish Episcopal Church reported that it has "the largest community of students for a generation or more was currently in training", a cohort of 27 of whom 5 were under 30. (Report in the *Church Times*, 17th June 2016.)

65. Op cit., Endnote 9, *UK Church Statistics* No 2, Table 1.1.1

66. *Pulling Out of the Nosedive*, A contemporary picture of churchgoing, Peter Brierley, Christian Research, London, 2006, Figure 8.6

67. Ibid., Table 8.3

68. See "The Optimum Length of Ministry" in op cit., Endnote 9, *UK Church Statistics* No 2, Page 17.4f

69. *Church Growth in the 1990s*, Research undertaken for Springboard, Peter Brierley, Christian Research, 2000

70. A Table drawn up of the variations in Table 6.1 and length in present appointment was found not to be statistically significant $[\chi^2 = 11.7, \nu = 9, P = 0.24]$

71. A Table was drawn up between the different groups, but it was not statistically significant for number of churches $[\chi^2 = 9.9, \nu = 6, P = 0.13]$ or for gender $[\chi^2 = 7.6, \nu = 9, P = 0.82]$

72. *God's Questions*, Peter Brierley, ADBC Publishers, 2008, Page 130

73. Quoted from *Prophetic Untimeliness*, A challenge to the idol of relevance, Os Guinness, Baker Books, Grand Rapids, Michigan, 2003, Page 103

74. Op cit., Endnote 66, *Nosedive*, Page 180

75. Op cit., Endnote 48, *Capital Growth*, Page 99

76. *Towards an Effective Deanery*, Peter Brierley, MARC Europe, 1990 for Methodist and Anglican Churches in East Anglia

77. Op cit., Endnote 48, *Capital Growth*, Page 100

78. In 2003 10% of English Baptist Churches were employing a Youth Worker, high by English standards then. *Annual Review Report*, Mission and Research Dept., Baptist Union of Great Britain, Page 2

79. 39.4% to 39.7% to one decimal place

80. Op cit., Endnote 16, *Turning the Tide*, Page 99

81. Church of Scotland, *Ministry among Young People*, Christian Research report, London, 2001, for Parish Education Department, Church of Scotland

82. Op cit., *Turning the Tide*, Endnote 16, Page 102

83. *Reformation, Dissent and Diversity*, The Story of Scotland's Churches, 1560-1960, Andrew T N Muirhead, Bloomsbury, London, 2015, Figure 1, Page 213

84. Given in *Religious Trends* No 2, 2000/2001, Christian Research, Eltham, London, 2000, Table 2.3, augmented by later figures from op cit., Endnote 66, *Nosedive*, Table 1.2 and extended to 2015

85. "The Father of Church Growth" in *India Church Growth Quarterly*, July-Sept 2014, Vol 21, No 2, Page 11

86. Article in *The Church of England Newspaper* by Dr Michael Moynagh, 27th May, 2016, Page 16

87. Published as *An analysis of fresh expressions of Church and church plants* begun in the period 1992 to 2012, Rev Dr George Lings, Church Army, October 2013

88. Such as provided by the newly-formed (2015) Scottish School of Christian Mission, for example

89. Op cit., Endnote 66, *Nosedive*

90. Assuming a similar percentage running an Alpha course among the churches not replying to the Census

91. It is not known how many churches running both Youth and

Adult Alpha courses ran Youth or Adult courses, but since overall on average churches ran almost 3 Adult Alphas to one Youth, the same proportion has been used for each denomination

92. Op cit., Endnote 1, *Church Statistics*

ABOUT BRIERLEY CONSULTANCY

B rierley Consultancy began in 2007, after its founder moved on from being the Executive Director of Christian Research for 14 years and European Director of MARC Europe for the 10 years prior to that. He has been the Lausanne Catalyst for Church Research since 1984. In 1972 he began what became in 1983 the *UK Christian Handbook* and when with Christian Research compiled 7 editions of *Religious Trends*. Brierley Consultancy is committed to:

- Building vision for the future for individual churches and Christian agencies.
- Interpreting the results from research and suggesting actions so that the Kingdom of God may grow.
- Enabling strategic thinking in churches or agencies using the latest analyses of Christian life in the UK and the rest of the world.

A 6-page bi-monthly bulletin called *FutureFirst* has been published by Brierley Consultancy since 2009, which aims to "provide facts for forward planning", a digest of contemporary statistical information on church and religious life. For a sample copy please write to the address below. It has received many plaudits from church and agency subscribers for its succinct but relevant articles.

Peter Brierley is known in the UK for organising and analysing large scale Church Censuses of church attendance held in the various countries of the United Kingdom, such as the 2005 English Church Census, the results of which were published in September 2006, though he was also responsible for the London Church Census in 2012. This is the report of the most recent, the fourth Scottish Church Census, in 2016.

Recent key publications include:

- *UK Church Statistics 2010-2020,* No 2, ADBC Publishers, August 2014. No 3, the 2018 edition, is in course of preparation to be published in 2017.
- *Hand in Hand,* the story of the first 20 years of the Kisumu Children Trust, 2015
- *Capital Growth* (what the 2012 London Church Census revealed), ADBC Publishers, June 2013
- *Major UK Religious Trends 2010 to 2020*, Brierley Consultancy, February 2011
- *God's Questions*, Vision, Strategy and Growth, ADBC Publishers, September 2010

Conferences especially for leaders of larger churches are organised each year, in association with CPAS. Peter is also a Trustee of several Christian charities.

The Consultancy happily works with all Trinitarian churches and organisations – Anglican, Methodist, Baptist, Presbyterian, Reformed, Independent, Catholic, Pentecostal, Charismatic, Orthodox and many smaller denominations. It does not work with non-Trinitarian groups such as the Jehovah's Witnesses or Mormons.

Brierley Consultancy is headed by Dr Peter Brierley, a statistician with over 50 years of experience in working on Christian evaluation, research and publishing. For more information please contact him at

The Old Post Office
1 Thorpe Avenue
Tonbridge
Kent TN10 4PW, UK
or by email: peter@brierleyres.com,
or phone +44 (0) 1732 369 303.
Website: www.brierleyconsultancy.com.
or www.scottishchurchcensus.com

INDEX